Vesna Maric was born in Mostar in 1976. She left Bosnia-Herzegovina when she was sixteen and came to Britain. She studied Czech Literature at the School of Slavonic and East European Studies, UCL in London and went on to work for the BBC World Service. She now writes Lonely Planet travel guides and a variety of journalism for publications including Time Out guides and BBC Online. An excerpt from *Bluebird* won a Penguin Decibel prize for new writing in 2007. Vesna Maric lives in London and is currently writing her first novel.

'This engaging memoir charts Maric's experiences as she tries to adjust to the British way of life. Vividly related vignettes range from dealing with patronising do-gooders to falling in love with a local boy, combining a personal coming-of-age tale with insight into the trials, strangeness and unexpected pleasures of the asylum seeker's lot. Charming, funny and moving. In short, a treat' *thelondonpaper*

'Her first impressions of Britain and the British are amusing, as are the clichéd expectations that British people have of her own country. The well-intentioned gestures of those selected to look after the new arrivals make for some pitiful scenes. There is a powerful story being told here' *Independent on Sunday*

'Humour is Maric's arsenal. From the moment she and her older sister say goodbye to their mother and board the crowded bus bound for the north of England the reader is treated

'Told with humour and defiance, this is the inspiring tale of a brave young woman' *Belfast Telegraph*

'The stories Maric tells are at once completely familiar and entirely alien . . . Maric's style is strong and direct and immensely readable. She conveys much in few words' *Bookbag.co.uk*

'War memoirs don't have to be grim reading. They can even be funny . . . [A] lively memoir' *Financial Times*

'Her confident, beguiling voice, her refusal to be pitied or patronised, reminds us that young people caught up in war have their own perspectives, their own stories to tell.' Marina Lewycka, *Guardian*

'Maric's sweetly personal memoir of her years as a refugee . . . is a salutary reminder not only that Bosnia was once ravaged by violence and hatred, but that a once-peaceful society was smashed to pieces in the process' *Time Out*

'[Vesna Maric is a] gifted, original writer . . . we are lucky to have her' *Observer*

Bluebird

A Memoir

Vesna Maric

GRANTA

Granta Publications, 12 Addison Avenue, London W11 4QR

First published in Great Britain by Granta Books, 2009
This paperback edition published by Granta Books, 2010

An excerpt from this book previously appeared, in a different form,
in *From Here to There: Sixteen True Tales of Immigration to Britain*,
published by Penguin Books, 2007.

A CIP catalogue record for this book
is available from the British Library.

1 3 5 7 9 10 8 6 4 2

ISBN 978 1 84708 119 3

Typeset by M Rules

Printed and bound in Great Britain by
CPI Bookmarque, Croydon CR0 4TD

To Rafael, my mother
and baby Ima,
with love

There'll be bluebirds over
The white cliffs of Dover,
Tomorrow, just you wait and see.

There'll be love and laughter
And peace ever after
Tomorrow, when the world is free.

The shepherd will tend his sheep,
The valley will bloom again
And Jimmy will go to sleep,
In his own little room again.

There'll be bluebirds over
The white cliffs of Dover,
Tomorrow, just you wait and see.

NAT BURTON

Contents

Bluebird

Good morning, neighbour

I remember a piece of TV footage that later became legendary. Demonstrators walking through the streets of Sarajevo suddenly ducked in an ensemble like long grass swaying in the wind. People looked around, bewildered, wondering what it was that had whizzed past their ears and made that girl fall so violently. A girl from Dubrovnik, a student, had been shot by a sniper on one of the bridges and her body lay stretched out on Sarajevo's scummy shallow river. She was the first victim of the war.

The snipers were hiding in the Holiday Inn, built eight years before for the 1984 Winter Olympics. At first the Holiday Inn had been regarded with affection. People had nicknames for it, like 'fried egg, sunny side up' because of its yellow façade that peeked through the thick snow in winter. Everyone went there for coffee on

Bluebird

Sundays. It was *the* place in town. During the war, the hotel housed foreign journalists, who sat through the night in the cold dark rooms, pondering the meaning of life and what they were doing there as the shells crushed and pockmarked the shivering city. And at the beginning of the war, in those same rooms sat the snipers who shot at the crowd beneath them on that sunny spring day. I watched it live on TV, with my family, in our living room in Mostar. The term 'reality TV' hadn't yet been invented.

When the girl fell, we gasped. My mother immediately telephoned her sister in Sarajevo in a panic. Checking that relatives and friends were alive was to become a dreaded, regular feature of our lives.

The radio was blaring an invitation to go into the streets. 'To win over the tyrants,' the presenter said. We'd already been demonstrating for days. 'Good morning, neighbour' was the new, humanist motto, pitching hard for a multi-ethnic Bosnia and Herzegovina. I was passionate about it and ran down the stairs into the street. That day the crowd was smaller. Machine-gun fire could be heard in the hills; I'd never heard it before. It sounded bizarre, real machine-gun fire; like the chattering of teeth, or a sewing machine worked by a master tailor. It was uncomfortable to realize that the chatter was now potentially lethal and not something heard only in American action movies. That day we went home earlier and the morning after no one said: 'Good morning, neighbour'.

This wasn't my first introduction to war, though. Some days before, on my way home from school, a tremendous explosion shook the city. Windows shattered around me, people screamed, the ground trembled and everyone ran in random directions. The war had started literally with a bang, and our world ended with the same noise that had started the world zillions of years ago. I didn't know what to do and instead of following my instincts and throwing myself on the floor (as in partisan films), I went home. I knocked on my neighbour's door and we tried to work out where the explosion had come from. We looked over the horizon from his terrace. There was smoke in the north of the city. He said: 'It must be the Northern Military Camp. That's where the smoke is coming from.' I nodded. I had no idea where the Northern Military Camp was and if what he was saying was true.

It was a cloudy spring day, the air was warm and we'd just started wearing short sleeves and drinking coffee outside. The flowers of the linden trees perfumed the streets and it was my favourite time of the year.

I headed towards my mother's shop, wanting to see what was happening in the city. People stood in huddles. There was confusion and everyone was saying something different. Snippets of conversations struck my ears: 'Don't trust anyone. Everyone's lying.' 'They say it was a cistern, full of petrol, the driver was still inside. He was baked. Still held the steering wheel in his hands, though. Must have been a good driver.'

I stopped by my best friend's house on the way. Her father, Mr Dušan, was in the army, so I thought he might be able to shine some light on the situation. Mr Dušan was a broad man. On that particular day he looked even broader than usual. And anxious. He sat at the kitchen table grappling with a crossword, and judging by the amount of scribbling, he was getting everything wrong.

'Will there be war, Mr Dušan?' I asked after making initial small talk and trying to think of a synonym for 'oil'.

'No, no, there won't be war, dear. It's just a bit of a mess, but nothing serious. Don't you worry,' he said. I still wonder if he was lying or whether he was really hoping it was going to come to nothing.

At my mother's shop customers speculated about what had happened. There, too, everyone had a different story. The only thing that was known for a fact was that a cistern had exploded near the Northern Military barracks. My neighbour had guessed right. People talked of a conspiracy by the army, or said that it was an accidental explosion, or that 'the enemy' had planted the cistern. Who was the enemy, I wondered, but didn't ask anything for fear of being bombarded by more theories. My mother's colleague served some coffee. He was a sweet man who would later perish in a prison camp.

Good morning, neighbour

The media gave conflicting information, and soon there was talk of 'disinformation' and how it was the main tool for stirring fear and hatred. 'Don't trust anything you hear. Disinformation can be deadly,' the man on the radio said.

Early next morning, I received a phone call. It was my friend, the daughter of Mr Dušan.

'My father told me to tell no one, but we're leaving town. He says it's only for a while, until things calm down. I'll be back soon. I had to tell you.'

I was devastated. 'You come back soon then. I'll miss you,' I said.

I put the phone down and got up to look out of the window, as if something on the outside would tell me whether there'd be war. She was one of the many Serbs who left the city that week and never came back. My Serb relatives also left town that week. We stayed behind and demonstrated for peace, like chickens waiting for someone to come and axe our heads off.

A storm swept across the city that day, painted the air Halloween orange and uprooted trees. I watched roof slates come down and smash on the street. It was a beautiful storm. Afterwards people said: 'It's a bad omen. There will be war,' and I wondered whether the fact that people were deserting the city in the middle of March, the explosion of the day before, nationalist propaganda, growing mistrust – whether these things weren't bad omens? Why pick the storm to hang your doom on?

Bluebird

In the evening, as I was inspecting the roots of a fallen oak in the street, another explosion sounded, near my house. A car had whizzed by and someone had thrown a hand grenade into a bar, sending everything up in smithereens. There were dead bodies in the street, wounded, screams, the wailing of ambulances and police cars. Years later I met someone who was in that car. He said he was on his way home when a friend stopped and offered him a lift. He got into the car and the friend said: 'We just have to drop something off beforehand.' He didn't think anything of it. They drove down the street, and a guy who sat in the passenger seat and whom he'd never seen before, or has seen since, rolled down the window. The car slowed and he tossed a bundle into the bar. The driver stepped on the accelerator and they drove off, leaving behind a roaring explosion. The man who had been on his way home didn't speak for a week after that.

The bar was a place where the army reservists hung out. Around that time many army reservists sprouted up in the streets, especially in bars. They were mainly older men in pine green crumpled and ill-fitting uniforms and carrying weapons. They belonged to so many different military and paramilitary organizations that you had no idea who they were half the time. They caused a lot of trouble, storming drunk into places and chasing everyone out, shooting into the walls with their worn-out AK47s.

There had been (and still was) trouble in Slovenia and

Croatia, but no one thought there would be war in Bosnia and Herzegovina. It was impossible. We loved each other. We wanted sovereignty, a multi-ethnic country. But then, after the general elections, it looked as if we didn't really love each other that much after all. Everyone loved only themselves and voted for their own nationalist party. The media were all saying something different and I stopped listening to the radio and watching the news. Disinformation, I remembered, spreads only fear and hatred.

After the bombing of the bar, my mother decided that the best thing would be to send my sister and me to Sarajevo. It was the capital, she said, nothing would happen there. The idea that Sarajevo would be safe was the common and inexplicable assumption of many people at the time. The next day we went to the train station and found out that all the trains were cancelled because of the barricades around Sarajevo. It was divine intervention, we later concluded, because two days after that the city was besieged. As shells pounded Sarajevo, my aunt was crying on the phone saying their house was right under the army base on the hill, where the shells were coming from. And it was almost impossible to escape.

Shelling started in Mostar too, and I woke up to a wailing general alert. It was a sound that went up and down like a dog howling at the moon. My mother ran through the house shouting: 'Come on, come on, get ready, we're going to the shelters.' We crumbled down the stairs and joined all our neighbours in the dark cellar where only coal, wood and mice had lived so far. There were old women with small transistors glued to their ears, children playing, unaware, mothers worried, and Olja, one of my neighbours, eight months pregnant. Men went in and out, discussing armaments and 'the defending of women and children'. Young men from the neighbourhood who had enrolled into the Territorial Army, a makeshift defence group made up of local men, came to show off their uniforms which consisted of camouflage trousers and one helmet to be shared between the three of them.

The spreading of disinformation continued. People kept coming into the shelter and saying things like: 'The army has broken through the defences and they are slaughtering everything in sight!' or 'There are reports of biological weapons in a village nearby! Everyone is dead!' Panic would stir the shelter, sending mothers into tears, while fathers wrung their hands and the old women's faces drooped into ever deepening scowls. They'd seen it all before.

Once a friend and I went for a coffee in one of the few bars that remained open. It was a quiet day and we wanted to do something that would make us feel normal. Afterwards we decided to go for a walk, but we were stopped by some people in the street. 'Where are you going?' they asked. 'For a walk,' we said. 'Are you crazy?' they shouted, looking terrified. 'There's fighting in the streets! Go home!' We went home even though the sky was so blue, with meringue clouds rolling across. The new spring leaves were every shade of green: emerald, toad, pea, mint. The park was creating fresh spring oxygen for us, and I thought of the darkness of the damp basement that awaited my return.

At home, my mother was sitting next to the radio crying. 'There's this man,' she sobbed, 'he's on the radio. He has taken control of the biggest dam in Bosnia and wants to blow it up if the army doesn't stop shelling his town.' I turned the volume up. Murat, the man in question, had called the national radio with his threat. The then president of Bosnia and Herzegovina, Alija Izetbegović, the then leader of the Yugoslav Army in Bosnia, General Kukanjac, and Murat's sister Fatima, had all been telephoned by the radio station for a live 'debate' and were on air. Murat claimed that he had 100 kilograms of explosives with him and that he was going to blow up the dam and drown half the country unless his demand was met. The problem was that the general was denying that his army was doing any shelling. Obviously, he was lying. The army was doing a lot of shelling.

On the radio, the president was trying to calm the angry Murat. 'Don't do it, Murat. Don't do it yet,' he said.

Bluebird

'What does he mean *yet*?' I asked my mother.

'I will do it, I will blow it up!' yelled Murat. His voice trembled.

Then his sister spoke: 'Murat, think of the people you would drown if you blow up the dam!'

'Well then Fatima, tell the general to stop shelling our town and killing our people,' responded Murat.

'Stop shelling, general,' said Fatima to the general in a stiff voice.

The general was defiant: 'We are not shelling anyone. That's someone else. We would not shell innocent people. Perhaps your people are shelling themselves and blaming us for it.'

I thought this was an ingenious theory, but Murat roared: 'Fuck you Kukanjac, you are a lying cunt!' live on national radio.

The general hung up and I clapped. It was a small but significant slap in the face of the Yugoslav Army from the people of Bosnia and Herzegovina. Someone recently remembered Murat, and we wondered what had happened to him. It turned out that he had no explosives, it was all a bluff.

We left town that day. Murderous shells flew in perfect arches, leaving 'pavement roses' in the asphalt. A pavement rose is a big hole with small holes radiating out in concentric circles. It looks a bit like a rose, but more like indelible vomit. They are our souvenirs from the war.

Good morning, neighbour

We were driven out of the city in a police car, by my mother's friend, a policewoman. As we passed through the deserted streets, the Serbian and Territorial Army soldiers (at that time, both Muslims and Croats) abused each other over their walkie-talkies, their fuzzy insults intercepted by the police radio:

'You motherfuckers, we're gonna crush your Islamo-Catholic skulls!'

Static.

'Your biggest poet, Njegos, died of syphilis. He fucked sheep up the arse.'

More static.

The car climbed up the hill and soon we could see the city unfold below. The radio was fading out.

The whole world seemed
to change

My mother had used bribery to get me to leave town without a fuss, by promising to let me go on holiday with friends to the seaside on my own. I fell for it and packed a small bag. 'A week only,' she said. But somehow, things got worse. My mother unintentionally made good her promise – we escaped to the Dalmatian coast, along with hundreds and thousands of others from Bosnia and Herzegovina and the warring parts of Croatia – and the exile turned into an interminable limbo similar to a cheerless holiday. I stayed at the seaside with my sister and my best friend for six months, while my mother alternated between Mostar, where my father had remained, and Dalmatia. The summer of 1992 had the gloomiest beach crowds in the world, and thanks to the abundance of worry and the sparseness of food, the skinniest of beach bodies. And although the prospect of returning home seemed further and further away, the war didn't feel real and I couldn't take it seriously. Surely, I thought, come September I would be starting school again and everything would be back to normal. Even the death toll, regular and increasing, broadcast on the radio news in a monotone, poetry-reading voice like T. S. Eliot's, seemed unreal.

And then one day the phone rang in the house where we were staying as refugees. We had been put up by one of the local families who opened up the musty rooms and echoing corridors of the upstairs floors reserved only for summer holidays and let us sleep there. We didn't get many phone calls. My uncle's panicked voice told me to hunt for my mother and not give up until I found her, that a terrible thing had happened, that my aunt had had an accident trying to leave town on an unlit road in the dead of night, that she was in a car with four other people, that no one else was hurt apart from her and that she might be dying. His voice was distorted in the old, plastic, grey phone receiver. While I listened, I wound the curly cord around my index finger until it was blue and slightly painful, to check the reality of the moment and to imprint it into my memory.

I ran and ran trying to find my mother, who had gone hunting for a room for us, our hosts having decided they'd had enough of refugees in their home. I discovered my first varicose vein as I ran up and down the one

15

street in the small seaside village, at first with great energy, but after a while with the step of a wounded soldier dragging an aching leg.

Apparently, my aunt had been found injured and motionless on the road somewhere near her home town, her spine cracked in three places. She was gathered up with care and transported to a hospital. The doctors, who always came to deliver bad news in the same way – rubbing their chins, stroking their noses or polishing their glasses with a small soft cloth – couldn't help her and kept sending her further and further away, to bigger and better hospitals around the country. We travelled for miles through ravaged cities and villages following her broken body from one hospital to another, until we eventually followed it to a graveyard. Some journeys we made on dust-ridden, stinky coaches, only the whites of our eyes visible in the black night. Some we made in the shells of cars with nothing but bare seats in them, scraping the ground with the hard tyres like nails on a blackboard. We sat inside these metal beasts, silent and slouched, as unsuspecting, swallowed victims, thin necked and wide eyed. Next to me on the last journey sat my mother enveloped in a black mourning shawl, sallow faced lips turned downwards, eyes red and vacant.

For months after her death, I kept convincing myself that my aunt was still alive and well, in her one-bedroom flat in eastern Bosnia, sitting at her sewing machine, cheerful and chatty, squinting through her half-moon glasses. Or that she was picking at the teeth of her latest denture creation – she was a dental technician, her flat always full of denture rubbers and false teeth – while soft snowflakes melted on the window panes. She used to sew clothes and make dentures for the whole family. As soon as someone lost their last real tooth biting on a hard apple, Aunt Mira would be there to press the rubbery mould into their jaws and create their future bright smile. I dreamed of going to pick wild strawberries in the woods near her house again and remembered her famous ice-cream cake, a thing so delicious I can still conjure up the sensation of it melting on my tongue and the feeling of impatience and reverence as we stood at the freezer door as if it were an altar.

When she died the whole world seemed to change. There were no more family holidays like those in the bleached photographs, she would never again beep outside the house as she parked her Renault 4 with the gear shift on the dashboard like racing cars. We wouldn't drive to the coast together, the children singing on the back seats, competing as to who would be the first to spot the sea ('Me, me, me!'). We wouldn't go to see her in wintertime, and sledge in the snow and skate on the frozen river.

The funeral was large and the sun beat hard on the line of mourners who moved slowly, like a dark serpent. The women in the front wailed, their arms locked together forming a wreath so you didn't know which arm belonged to whom. They held each other, some fainting with grief, others wiping their tears with small white handkerchiefs. My grandmother had a single tear glittering on her cheek, thanking God that we could at least bury the body with dignity, unlike so many other poor families who never found the bodies of their relatives. Given the circumstances, I suppose my grandmother was right. We were lucky in a perverted sort of way. We had to be grateful for being granted the chance to honour my aunt's memory. Family members each took a handful of black earth and threw it on the polished coffin. The soil thudded bluntly and spilled to the sides.

During the funeral my mother mentioned there was an opportunity to go to Britain. She said that there was a convoy, women and children only, and that my sister and I should go. 'What about you?' I asked. 'I'll stay here,' she said, and when she saw my face fill with terror, added: 'It would only be for six months. Not for ever, silly.' I was not encouraged by the shortness of time for I understood that time meant nothing and circumstance everything. I didn't want to think of the danger I would be escaping and my mother would be facing. Things at home were rotten, I wanted to get out. But if I left, was I betraying, was I deserting them all? And what would become of me? For days after, I listened to the heart-wrenching male warble of a popular song on the radio: 'I am never leaving this city, everything that is mine remains here' and tortured myself. Should I leave my family, my language, my culture, my childhood, my friends, my everything? Or should I stay and try to fight? Or become a nurse? I could get out until things got better, improve my English and then come back. For sure. And then I could be a nurse.

I often wonder what would have happened if I had decided to stay in Bosnia. What would I be now? I could have been anything: a mother sitting in front of the TV with two kids at her side; a secretary filing her nails and huffing while she looks at the clock; a successful businesswoman; a corpse, lying beneath a black marble stone bearing my name and dates of birth and death; an NGO worker; a flower girl.

We moved into my grandmother's house in a small Herzegovinian village and waited for the departure date to arrive. I watched the days pass slowly, weeks stretching like blind caterpillars.

Grandma

My grandmother's house was a dwarfy white box with one room, a triangular attic and a low grey ceiling. Mice ran around the attic, among the wheat and the corn, and you could hear their small feet trickle above your head. On the ceiling, flies stood upside down rubbing their legs. They buzzed around in concentric circles, and settled down in the darkness when my grandma went to sleep. She sat on her bed during the day with her plastic fly-swatter erect and squashed the flies without turning her head, without looking, like a karate master.

My grandma wore a black long-sleeved dress with tiny buttons down the front, and a black shawl under which two grey plaits were wrapped around her head like pretzels. Sometimes she took the shawl off and combed her thin hair and I watched. She'd worn black ever since my

20

grandfather died in 1980, as a sign of eternal mourning and widowhood, which is what the women in the village were supposed to do when their husbands died. She had lived in the small house for the last sixty years, which is how old the mulberry tree outside was, the tree she had planted when they moved in. She died in her early nineties (nobody really knew how old she was because nobody was really sure when she was born), in pretty good shape, both mentally and physically. She had had eight children, dozens of grandchildren and several great-grandchildren by the time she died, and she remembered everyone's name.

My grandma was Catholic and she prayed every day, even though she'd never read the Bible. I knew this because she was illiterate. She still owned reading glasses, though, which she used when she was knitting. She was an amazing knitter – she made slippers or the belts that Franciscan monks wore around their brown robes, the white ropes that look like curtain ties. She knitted them with eight needles, in deadly concentration, her thick reading glasses balanced on her nose. Her sight was still pretty good even at ninety-something.

I once tried to teach grandma to write. I was about seven and wanted her to be able to read the newspapers, not just look at the pictures all the time, so I took a pencil and a piece of paper, wrapped my hand around hers and started shaping the letters. The grey lead bled a crooked A,

Bluebird

a swollen B, a hunchbacked C. She did it for a while, probably just to humour me, but one day she decided that she'd had enough. She realized it wasn't just something I was going to do for a couple of days before I got bored, that I was really keen on teaching her. So she said: 'Sorry kid, but I can't do this, I'm too old. I get a headache.'

After that, when we went to see grandma at weekends, I would catch flies from the ceiling, pull off their wings, put them in a matchbox and watch them trying to crawl out. I used a magic method for catching them. It only worked with flies that were resting on the ceiling. I'd fill half a glass with water, adding a little olive oil that settled on top, and press the rim on the ceiling, encircling the fly. The insect would surrender to the oily liquid, diving into it head first, as if it were the only thing it had ever wanted to do.

My mother says that when she was a teenager, grandma was very strict. She didn't let the girls go on dates. My mum was the youngest of the eight children and she always says she felt that she didn't really have a mother, that she could never talk to grandma about her problems or ask for advice because she was so strict. Once she went on a date with some boy from the village, wearing a short skirt, and grandma chased her with a cane and whipped her bare legs in front of her date. She never saw the boy again, of course. My mother was a teenager in the sixties and a young woman in the seventies, when women were supposed to be liberated. But there was no liberation in the village. So my mum left the village and sought work and liberation in the city.

It was different with grandpa. He used to give my mother money and let her go out whenever she wanted. I remember him sitting by the window, looking at the road, wearing a black beret. He smoked tobacco that he grew himself. When I was very small I used to get up with him early in the morning to collect the dry tobacco leaves off the ground where they basked in the sun, and stick a large rusty needle through them, stringing them on to a thick thread and hanging them on the wall. They smelled musty and sweet.

When grandma prayed, it was in a whisper. She moved the rosary through her fingers, feeling its texture. It was impossible to interrupt her when she prayed. I tried many times. I would ask her things or tell her jokes, or sad stories, but she would just ignore me. Sometimes she would stop for a second, spit into her handkerchief, and then carry on moving her muted lips, an occasional fricative escaping her mouth.

When the war started, it was my grandma's third. She was born around 1912 and was a child during the First World War. In the Second World War she was already a married woman with children and was living in the small house with grandpa. During that war my grandpa buried their sewing machine, so that the partisans or the

Germans or whoever wouldn't come and steal it. He dug it up in 1945 in perfect condition and everyone talked about it for years. My grandma used to show me the slogan written by the partisans in red paint on the wall at the front of the house that read 'FREEDOM FOR ALL'. Now you can't see it any more because it's been whitewashed, but if it rains a lot the red letters bleed through.

In spring 1992 my grandma had not left the village in fifty years, except for two short stays with us in Mostar. There was talk of the village being invaded and everyone being moved to the coast for a while, but she didn't want to go. In the past, every time she left the house for longer than a day or two, she fell ill. My mother convinced her that it would only be for a short time, that she would come back soon, and that it was dangerous for her to stay. So she budged and went to the coast, where my mum, sister and I were staying. She was housed in a hotel, part of which was a makeshift old people's home. They were all from different villages and missed their daily work, and none of them enjoyed staying in a hotel at the seaside. We used to joke with them when we went to see grandma: 'Come on, this is great for you – it's the first time you've had a real holiday! You're in a hotel, the beach is at your doorstep, and all you have to do is go for a swim every day!' They would just wave a hand limply, sigh and carry on looking out of the window with watery eyes. In her hotel room, my grandma was ill. She had fallen sick the day she arrived. 'It's been a month. Nothing is happening in the village. I want to go home,' she kept saying.

One day a general alert sounded in the seaside town and all the old people at the hotel had to go down to the shelters. There was confusion on the stairs, Zimmer frames forgotten, dentures left bobbing in a glass on a bedside table. When the alert ended, none of the old people knew how to get back to their rooms. They had no idea what number their room was or what floor they were on. They crammed the stairs, with wrinkled hands clutching the handrails, eyes enlarged behind thick glasses, scanning each other's faces for a clue. After that, my grandma threatened to die if we didn't take her home. Her condition worsened, she was confined to her bed and my mother, scared that she would die out of spite, took her back to the village. She recovered immediately.

Soon afterwards we went to stay with her. Of the months between saying the historical 'yes' and leaving, I remember everything through a film of dust. The colour of the air in the upstairs rooms of my grandmother's house was pale ochre, and my mother and I had a rat for a companion and a broken black and white TV for entertainment. The TV poured soap operas from its screen and I immersed myself in their foam, followed their meaningless affairs to get away from the knowledge I was leaving and kissing my childhood goodbye. I wanted to fool the feeling that my life would never be the same again.

The gathering of people

The day we left was a hot September morning, after a night of torn sleep. A crowd of seventy or eighty people stood on the seafront, besieged by suitcases, getting ready to board the two coaches. We were mainly women and children. The men were waiting around to say good-bye to their wives; a couple had managed to evade the draft somehow and were coming along. My sister and I stood with our distraught mother, watching the playful ripples of the Adriatic. Outside the two double-decker buses, busying around and already a little red from the autumn sun, were the British. They had come to take us away from our dusty old towns where things had not been so good lately.

The journey had been cooked up through a children's organization by Dragan, in association with Peter, a man from the north of England. Dragan worked in a steel factory before the war broke out and he was now in charge of us – a 'manager', as he liked to be known. None of us knew exactly where we were going. All that Dragan had told us was to dress down and look as bedraggled as possible, because the previous group, he said, was too dressed up. The British had complained they didn't really look like refugees. Dragan had described it to my mother the week before, over the telephone: 'They looked as if they were dressed for a wedding!' I imagined my vain compatriots in their Italian fashion suits rescued from their homes, lipstick and eye shadow intact, like armour.

The British had, understandably, expected something a little more like 'proper' refugees: people suffering, hardship visible on their faces, clothes torn and wrinkled, children's eyes crusted with tears. Dragan wove through the crowd, closely inspecting everyone's outfits by pinching a shirt, a skirt or a trouser between two fingers, rubbing it to feel its quality, a look of disgust on his face. It seemed we were well below standard. But the unspoken motto of these Bosnian mothers was: 'If we are going to be refugees, let's not advertise our misery, let us at least look good,' and I could understand how they felt. It's not easy suddenly becoming a refugee.

I had struggled with the idea. I had spent my entire life being just me, belonging to a family, judged mainly by my freckly face or dodgy relatives. But I had never been pitied before, until the word 'refugee' was uttered. I was only sixteen and without preconceptions of what being a refugee meant. But here I was, about to become a 'foreigner'. My entire life was going to change.

The time came for my sister and me to board the coach, a time still too sore to remember. My mother's face was flooded by my rivers of tears, and between us a smeared window pane stood like a symbol of our separation. The bus perhaps smelled of England and I thought I would never see my mother again, or smell the Adriatic sea that framed her curled hair. The engine grumbled, not wanting to move from the comfort of the sun.

There were children on the bus, making posters that read: 'We are the Bosnian refugees!', 'Bosnia and Herzegovina ♡ England!' and 'We love Penrith!' I asked the children if they knew where Penrith was. They said: 'No' and continued to draw a picture of a bus that was supposed to resemble the one we were on, holding on to the white paper with little fingers stained with red, green and blue marker pens. I faced the asphalt unwinding before us, trying to avoid looking at anything that might make me cry, like trees, mountains or the sea.

Dragan and the lady who
never left the house

Dragan was a factory manager and an amateur poet with a cigarette permanently hanging out of the side of his mouth, ashing on his shoes and sweater. He had a collection of jumpers, all with diamond patterns and V necks; his dark chest-hair protruded over the root of the V as if curious to see the world. His hair was swept over his egg-shaped head and his yellowing, nicotine complexion made it look as if the sun were permanently setting on him. He was in his fifties, his eyes always in a squint, cigarette smoke stinging them, the smoke which, some ten years later, would give him lung cancer and kill him in a hospital in North London.

Dragan wrote poems about unrequited love, was sentimental and had had a love affair with a woman who was known in my home town as 'the woman who never left her house'. Attracted by the mystery, he arranged to meet her, posing as a journalist who wanted to write a piece about her for a local newspaper. After he left her house that day he began writing her love poems, thinking up sonnets as he crossed the bridge over the foaming green river. She was reputedly a beauty, with hair that stretched to the floor and breasts that looked up at the sky. Her mother, aware of her immense beauty and herself betrayed by 'vagabond men', as she called them, was worried she might attract the wrong sort of suitor, and swore her daughter never to leave the house until she got married. She kept her promise, but because she never trusted any man enough to let him meet her daughter, the woman stayed in the house permanently. After her mother died, she was so used to being inside and so afraid of the outside that she simply carried on as before.

Soon after Dragan's first visit, the whole town realized they were having an affair because he was always going to her house. It's hard to conduct an affair with someone who refuses to leave their house and go to a secret, hidden place. There are many such locations in my home town, hidden I mean, only not so secret because everyone knows about them, since most of those who have affairs use the same places. Then they keep their knowledge about the other adulterers like revolvers at their hips, ready to shoot the information about each other at any time.

Dragan's wife was unhappy about it because it made

her look like a fool, but deep down she didn't mind. He was not an attractive man and he became difficult when he drank (which he did often), and she preferred him spending more time away from her. Plus, she too was having an affair, with my doctor. I knew this because Dragan and his wife lived in our building and every time the doctor finished examining me for my juvenile arthritis he would say: 'Don't you live in the same building as Mrs D?' and when I said yes, he'd give me some dried lavender to deliver to her. He always used some transparent excuse for sending her the stuff, mentioning winter clothes and moths and good wardrobe-keeping. I would take the stiff, parched lavender – the doctor's desiccated, aromatic love – between my swollen fingers, occasionally smelling the fragrant purple flowers.

The woman who never left her house didn't venture outside even during the war. Before the war her groceries and other necessities were brought to her by the kind people who worked in the shops near her home. She never needed to work because her mother had left her quite a fortune after her death. But once the war started no one was going to bring her supplies any more. There was no running water, and people had to queue at street water-pumps, clutching their most prized possession of the time: plastic containers. Nobody wanted to risk their life bringing her food and water, because the sniper alleys leading to her house were too dangerous. And there was nowhere for her to hide during the shelling sprees because her house had no basement. But not even Dragan's love could overcome the stubbornness, agoraphobia, martyrdom or whatever it was that kept her so firmly indoors. It proved impossible for her to get her foot over the doorstep when Dragan and the others tried to make her get out and save her life.

After Dragan had given up on her, he went back to his wife and two sons and started organizing escape routes manically for everyone else. Perhaps he was compensating for the fact that he couldn't convince the woman he loved to leave her house at last, to save her own life, so he made it his business to get as many others as possible to listen to his advice and get out of the country. They say her house was flattened in the early stages of the three-year war.

Gordana's secret

We all wondered if the English were being paid for this job, but it turned out they were volunteers, ordinary people moved to do something about what they saw on TV. I admired their ability to act. I repeatedly heard people saying how they wanted to work with the poor, help the world, the elderly, the unwanted, but I didn't know anyone who had actually given up the comfort of their lives to do so.

It seemed to me that we, the victims, and they, the rescuers, would have perfectly defined roles, and I imagined us swimming together in the comforting sea of empathy. I didn't yet understand what I came to understand later – that between a rescuer and a victim stands human nature and aside from empathy, there are self-righteousness, expectations, self-fulfilment, and roles which at first are defined and clearly demarcated often become muddled and intertwined.

Gordana's secret

A few hours into the journey some of us were in need of a cigarette. Gordana was a mother of two who looked like Xena, the Warrior Princess, with a tight dark plait snaking down to her steely buttocks hugged by a pair of lilac leggings. She guided the smokers up to the bus's roof window. With one jerk of her muscular arm, she yanked the handle and propped the window up on its black metal legs. The air blew our hair around, and the smoke danced a speedy wiggle before escaping upwards. We wondered if we were allowed to smoke. 'Of course we're allowed, we're in distress,' Gordana said. The sky sped above us and layered clouds, fluffy dog, bear and dragon shapes, stretched across the blue. Gordana's hair was steady against the wind, black and tight across her skull, the parting in the middle like the deep bed of a dry river. Below it was a small forehead and big, heavily mascaraed eyes. She blinked slowly and inhaled deeply, sucking the orange cigarette filter with purple lips. The lipstick had bled into the small wrinkles around her mouth. She exhaled the smoke and watched it leave the bus through the window, slowly curling upwards at first, and then being violently yanked by the hurrying wind. The cigarette rested between her purple nails, long and curving downwards. Purple is obviously her colour, I thought.

She started talking suddenly, in a nasal drone. She was in trouble, she said. The other women gathered round to hear better, their smoke and sorrow mingling with ours. Gordana said that she had been menopausal for some months now, her periods were irregular, her moods swinging and hitting anyone passing by. Her skin was drying faster. 'You've got to watch it, girls,' she said to us younger ones, 'you'd better make sure you live healthily, not smoking like this, you're still young but time goes fast.' She took another drag, the cigarette's ember eating up the paper quickly, crackling.

'C'mon Gordana, what's the trouble about?' said one of the women.

'Well, I thought since I was entering menopause and all that, I would get rid of the coil that I used as a contraceptive. This was around three or four months ago. And you know, me and my man, we still have sex quite often. We fuck every which way, whenever we can. It's always been like that, ever since we met. Sure we fight too, plates against the walls, coffee stains all over the place, but we make up. I thought I was too old to get pregnant. I'm fifty-two. Who the hell gets pregnant at fifty-two?' She stopped, took another drag. As she continued, smoke came out of her mouth and nostrils, rolling over her tongue. 'Well, *I* get pregnant at fifty-two. And I just found out this morning, before we got on this fucking bus.'

'Are you sure?' somebody asked.

'I bought a test last night. My period was late but I

thought it was normal, being menopausal and all, until I started getting morning sickness. I know when I'm pregnant, you know what I'm saying?' Everyone nodded, even me, although I had no idea how it is to feel pregnant.

'I was too scared to do it last night, but this morning when I puked again I thought I'd better piss on this thing and get it over with. Misko was still there and I thought it'd be better to do it while he was there, you know, for moral support. He waited outside the toilet door at the bus station. The blue lines appeared next to each other and I thought: fiftyfuckingtwo, pregnant, refugee, leaving husband behind, menopausal, having an abortion. Fuck me. What the fuck am I doing?'

'Oh, Gordana. That's really shit, man.'

Everyone nodded, tut-tutted, shook their heads. Gordana's eyes started streaming with tears, bubbles of saliva gathered in the corners of her mouth as she wept. The women gave her a hug and a pat on the back, 'there, there'. Her purple-nailed fingers wiped away the tears and smeared the thick mascara, the whites of her eyes turned red, and her lipstick was a bruise on her flushed, sobbing face. I went to my seat to get her a handkerchief.

We looked after her in various ways for the rest of the journey. One of the older girls, who spoke good English, explained what was going on to one of the English women and it was rumoured that Gordana was to have an induced miscarriage once we arrived in England.

Apparently after Gordana took the pill, it hurt a lot. I imagined her bleeding the baby out of her womb, terrified and grateful.

Hiroshima mon amour

The journey proceeded uneventfully for the most part. I was busy writing letters and listening to my Walkman, arguing with my sister about whose turn it was to sprawl across the other. A cooling stream of air came out of the egg-shaped ventilation hole above my head and I moved it around the way a chameleon moves his eye, in short bursting movements, to annoy my sister. The children were also getting restless, one of them always intent on stripping off naked. Her mother commented that she must have been a stripper in her past life because she hated wearing clothes. Every time her mother succeeded in getting her dressed, the little girl would whip her shirt off over her head, leaving her hair standing with static, and dance out of her trousers.

The video *The Snowman* – the only children's video on the bus – was played over and over again until we all,

39

children, adults and those of us in between, knew it off by heart. The haunting thin voice of the boy ('We're walking in the air . . .') filled our pores. The song drifted in and out of my dreams, and every time I looked up at the TV screen I'd see the boy and the snowman flying, happy, scarves flapping behind them. I begged secretly: 'Fall, fall, little snowman and boy, fall and die!' Still, to this day, my hair stands on end if I happen to hear that glassy voice.

One day, the organizers decided to surprise us by playing a different video. We were delighted. It started with pictures of a city with a green river, green trees, smiling people. I recognized my home town. A voiceover began: 'Once, Mostar was a beautiful, peaceful city. Its inhabitants lived happily alongside each other, regardless of their different ethnicities and religions. But then, the hatred that simmered for centuries, once again rose to destroy brother and neighbour.' Reels of shelling followed, houses crumbling like plaster models, trees screaming in the flames, people running, the city swallowed by fire, by hatred, by doom. It was a perfect action movie. I half expected John Rambo to appear on the screen, bare chested, pecs oiled and tense, an olive-coloured bandanna tight across his tanned forehead. It seemed absurd, perverse almost, that this video was being played on the same machine as *The Snowman*. What was going on? Where was the snowman and what did he think of this? Perhaps he was going to appear on the screen, himself bare chested, pecs oiled and tense, an olive-coloured bandanna tight across his icy forehead, sacrificing his frozen body by throwing himself on a burning house to extinguish the flames and rescue civilians from certain death?

I noticed Emma, one of the English volunteers, a small bird-like lady, weeping on the stairs of the bus. Tears dropped from her face on to her denim knees. She pushed her heavy glasses up and looked at the TV. I wondered why they thought it was a good idea to show this? Did we not look sufficiently upset? Perhaps it was like a motivational video, played to company employees to help them remember what they were there for? Were the English disappointed with us? I never understood. I looked at the others; no one protested. Some slept, some watched, some cried whilst watching.

Coffee

We spent nights of interrupted sleep at Esso petrol stations. I would wake up and see the red, white and blue neon glaring at me. For the first few seconds, I wouldn't know who or where I was. I would look around at the sleeping faces of my co-passengers, their heads hanging like wilting flowers, necks slackened by sleep. Some seemed to be dreaming about something nasty, their faces grimacing; others were more peaceful. The silence on the bus was calming. I looked out of the steamy window at the occasional cars shooting past, their small red lights leaving a fiery trail behind them.

The morning was filled with the stink of petrol, traffic fumes and dusty seats. A redolence of coffee struggled on to the bus. The small kitchen that was part of the second bus was visible through the window, but I could see only an arm vigorously stirring a beige liquid and tapping the

42

teaspoon on the edge of the cup as if about to conduct an orchestra. Our first English coffee was received with ungrateful spits and shouts of: 'This is not coffee! This is piss!' Instant coffee was weak and served in massive cups (I later learned they were called 'mugs', like ugly faces and robbing) and the British laughed in embarrassment. A few people pretended they liked the coffee, so as not to offend our hosts, saying: 'It tastes like tea!', grappling for appropriate cultural references. We were used to Turkish coffee, small and strong, coffee that tastes like petrol, clings to your palate for hours afterwards and sticks to the floor if you spill it. As soon as we arrived in Penrith, the Bosnian women said: 'Now we'll show you *our* coffee!'

They lined up as in an army canteen, whipped out the manual coffee grinders, the beans, the copper coffee pots and their small cups, similar to those used for sipping Japanese sake. The English sat and waited with smiles of anticipation.

Bosnian coffee is ground in the long copper tube grinder, an old-fashioned tool placed on the hip and gripped tightly. The other hand grabs the metal handle on top, and the grinding begins. The process lasts at least ten minutes, and it takes a firm bicep. The smell of copper then lingers on the palms, and whiffs at you as you bring the coffee cup to your lips.

One of my favourite childhood memories is of my

auntie's friend who looked like one of the Slav women depicted in those large communist paintings, only there the woman is usually wielding a flag, not a coffee grinder. This friend of my auntie was big and strong, with a white headscarf tied around wide cheekbones, eyes deeply set, an apron across broad hips, a shirt buttoned over bursting breasts. On her living-room door a round sticker read: 'We don't swear in this house', provided by the local Catholic church. Someone else must have stuck it there, because the family swore colourfully. I loved the ease with which she ground coffee, her brown arms strong, the muscles bulging under the rolled-up sleeves. My small arms still thin and weak on my skinny body, I dreamed of the day I would be able to grind the coffee so easily. I tried sometimes with grunts and puffs to do it myself – this being the ultimate test of strength – but the impatient coffee drinkers would take the grinder away from me and send me off to play with an empty one.

The Bosnian women had beads of sweat on their brows from preparing the coffee. They laughed like witches above the boiling thick black liquid that looked like the earth's very core. They were sure it was going to be a success with the English hosts, and after they proudly served it, they sat down and waited to see the results. The English, like most first-timers, burnt their fingers when trying to lift the cups (which come without holders), but the Bosnians demonstrated: 'Like this, like this', and held the cup with half a thumb and the tip of the index finger. The English slurped and coughed and then everyone laughed and oohed and aahed with delight.

Paris

Italy and Switzerland went past as if they were mere neighbourhoods. I remember Italy by a small black Fiat huffing uphill. In Switzerland I bought a black lighter with golden hieroglyphics and *viens avec moi* written on it. I had no idea what it meant, but it was a souvenir, and helped me pretend this was just a tourist trip.

One morning in France, on the third day of our journey, tired and cold, I got out of the bus for, a cigarette. As I stepped on the gravel, luminous white fog, thick like cotton wool, enveloped me. I walked towards a small path, wide enough for one car, to stretch my legs. There was an old road sign, the paint on it was peeling, and the hanging letters read PARIS. I smoked and wondered how far it was down this road and if I started to walk now, when I would make it. Everything around me was asleep.

Esma

A woman called Esma translated for us. Her English was remarkable because she had worked as an interpreter before, back in the old Yugoslavia. She had been to Britain many times and for us, she embodied the secrets of the land that awaited. She stood at the front of the bus like a tour guide, her curly afro hairdo partly blocking the windscreen, and we listened with intensity to every word she said. She spoke to us of strange English things like separate taps (*hot and cold, separate?! how strange! don't they get scalded first thing in the morning?*), driving on the other side of the road (*oh, I could never do that* – said the drivers – *I couldn't shift the gears right!*), double-decker red town buses (*ha ha ha* – we laughed – *like on the postcards*).

There was a middle-aged man among us who had escaped the country and the military draft God knows how, with a beard that seemed to envelop his entire face save for the top of his head, which was balding. His tiny dark eyes darted above a potato nose. He sat on one of the seats right in the middle of the bus. I suspect he did this on purpose, so that everyone could see and hear him when he started one of his lectures on just about any subject that came up. His name was Boban and he appeared to have had a variety of professions, from mathematician to art historian to optician. And of course, he knew everything there was to know about Britain and insisted on sharing his knowledge, even though we were more interested in Esma's interpretation of English customs.

So on the subject of taps, Boban would say: 'Oh yes, the taps. Well, do you know why they have these separate taps? (nostrils flaring) Do you know why they haven't opted for the marvels of modern bathroom design? (looks like he is going to burst) Eh?' He would look around at the despairing crowd. 'It is because it is their *tradition*. They have no other tradition they can be proud of, so *this* is their tradition! Ha ha ha!'

Soon we became afraid of discussing any subject and refrained from having group conversations, which of course didn't stop him eavesdropping on others' private exchanges and butting in with an opinion. Once he finally noticed that no one was interested, he started talking to the English, in his heavily accented voice, trying to stick a multi-syllable word at any point possible. 'I think

Esma

it is superfluous that the identification card is not in the existence in Britain! How do you expect to apprehend they who do not have desire for wellbeing of your homeland? What about, how do you say, tracking down a suspect?' The English, eternally polite, would smile, nod and discuss. Our interpreter and fellow refugee Esma became less and less inclined to translate things from one language to the other.

This Esma, the women chattered, was coping badly with the journey. She hadn't wanted to leave Bosnia. She had two daughters – they were on the bus with us – sweet little girls, all pigtails and smiles. The women, whose jaws worked on any piece of gossip with evident delight, and who longed for a hint of juicy morsels from other people's lives as a child longs for sweeties, spat out the tale, chewed and broken down by acidic gossip enzymes, any goodness gone out of it. The story was that Esma was used to her mother look- ing after the girls while she and her husband were off 'gallivanting around the city' and that now her husband was in the army fighting, and she was here, stuck with her daughters, having to take care of them and not knowing what to do. She couldn't cook, clean, wash; she could do nothing a Bosnian woman was supposed to be able to do with her eyes closed. I imagined her and her husband 'gallivanting'. (Where could you gallivant around our home town? You could hardly go for a walk.) And I imagined the girls playing at their grandma's, forgotten by *mama* and *tata*.

Bluebird

Whatever the truth about Esma and her husband and their parenting skills, she slowly turned from our eloquent translator at the front of the bus, microphone in hand and glasses balanced on the top of her nose, to a woman falling apart. She cried constantly. She started chain smoking and speaking in a speeded up, nervous way. Various doctors were called in to try to help. All she ever said was that she was worried about her husband, that she couldn't live if he died, and that she had to go back home. The girls watched their mother lose her mind slowly, her sanity unravelling like a bandage, leaving behind a chattering stranger they couldn't relate to. The women watched their co-passenger, tut-tutting away, eyebrows raised.

After she got to England even a spiritual healer was called in to help. She accused him of trying to touch her up, and made a huge scene; everyone was embarrassed by her, looking at the floor, the walls, the ceiling, anywhere away from her madness. By the time they took her to a psychiatrist, she was already *too far gone* – that was the expression used to describe her condition. The doctor said that there was nothing better to be done for her than to send her back to Bosnia, where she wanted to be. And that's what they did. Her daughters stayed in England, with an English family, and I have no idea what happened to them after that.

I heard nothing about Esma after she went back, and I

often remembered her, especially after I'd suffered my own bouts of depression later on. The memory of her frightened me, the thought that I could end up like her made me panic and buck up, not give in, not become unravelled, without a centre.

Years later I went back to visit my home town, which by then looked like no more than a cavity in the jaws of the world. It was summer time and sweltering heat radiated from the stone, the pavements, the walls. I was having an evening drink with a friend on a bar terrace. Shrieks and chattering made me turn around, and I saw a woman with an afro hairdo, big round glasses, wearing a loose white cotton dress. She was sitting at a table alone, smoking a cigarette, another four in the ashtray, freshly lit, creating a cosy little campfire. She laughed at the thin air sitting next to her in a yellow plastic chair. My stomach seized up with anxiety and I asked my friend if he knew who she was. I knew it was Esma, of course, but she had been confined to a sad, bad memory for a decade and I couldn't believe she was now sitting before me. 'Her name is Esma, she lives just down the road,' he answered, 'comes here every day and the waiters let her sit around while there's no customers. They say she went crazy during the war because she was raped and her children killed. Bad stuff.'

There she was, sharing a table with her imaginary

friends. Who was she picturing around her? Was it us, the people from the bus? Was it possible she would remember me? I said: 'She was with me in England. She lost her mind there. From loneliness I think. Couldn't hack it. I don't think she was raped. It happened quite quickly. You can't believe how fast the mind can be lost.'

I got up and approached her slowly, as if she were a wild animal and I didn't want to betray my fear. 'Esma?' I said. I don't know what I was trying to do. She looked up, eyeballed me suspiciously. 'Remember me? We went to England together. On the bus. You interpreted.' For a moment she seemed to recollect something, nose scrunched up to hold her heavy glasses as she focused, arm lifted to block out the light coming from a bulb behind me. 'Do you have a cigarette?' she said, her face half shadow under the hand that blocked out the light. I gave her my entire pack. She picked out a cigarette with a long nail and returned the rest. I stood above her, staring. I wanted her to remember, as if that might reverse the process and she'd collect her scattered mind again. But she went back to her friends and ignored me. I returned to my table. The ice had melted in my glass. 'What'd she say? Did she remember you?' asked Vedran. 'No. She asked for a fag.'

Welcome to Britain

On the fourth day of our journey we stood on the large ferry that bobbed on the waves of the Channel. The peeling paint of the rails stuck to our sweaty palms as we stared at the foam below. Johnny, the driver, had parked the bus downstairs alongside the other vehicles stacked up in the ferry's belly and came upstairs, stretching and shaking off a mild shiver. 'Welcome to England!' he said. 'It's bloody freezing!' and smoothed his frayed moustache over a smile. We stood next to each other like pigeons trying to warm up, ruffled by the gusts of the wind. All I could think of was the Vera Lynn song: 'There'll be bluebirds over/The white cliffs of Dover/ Tomorrow, just you wait and see . . .' I'd heard the song on Yugoslav radio some years before and I loved the melody. I taped it on an old cassette player, listened to it obsessively (as was my habit with songs in English), weeding out words I didn't understand and tracking them down in my thick English–Serbo-Croat dictionary. And though I couldn't see bluebirds anywhere, the white cliffs of Dover were becoming visible on the other side, brooding above the grey water and greeting us as if we were Dunkirk evacuees. I watched the outline of the white rocks blend with the sky.

We flooded into Dover immigration office, a drab, cold waiting room with tiled walls and bleak lighting. There were orange plastic chairs and a poster reminding us of what not to do. A man with a face like a scrunched up fist emerged out of an office. He squinted at his clipboard through thick glasses and gave us forms to fill in. Our English hosts helped us through them and those of us who had some English translated for those who had none.

My sister went into a room that had 'Interviews' written on it in black letters and answered questions about being my guardian – she was nineteen years old – what she was planning to do in the UK, what nationality we were. Mug shots were taken and stapled on to a document called 'IND' (which stood for Immigration and Nationality Department); one for each of us. Underneath our photos stood our names, already foreign and bald without the diacritics, and beneath were the dates and our near-incinerated places of birth, followed by a country that had ceased to exist. The IND document was our only proof of ID for years to come; it was something that either identified us as more work to weary or indifferent social service officials or denoted a person who was a potential black hole for any bank's funds. We were told we were not to leave the UK if we wanted our asylum claim to remain intact and our invalid Yugoslav passports were taken away. No one told us how long the claim would take to process, which, in my case, turned out to be four years.

Each person went in for their own interview, except for those who were minors, like me. And after they came out, we hurled thousands of questions at them, 'What did they ask you?' and 'What did you say?', as if there were a right and wrong answer. The old people in the crowd prayed and the children ran around; their parents dragged them back to their laps absentmindedly, hypnotized by anxious chatter.

Several hours later we rolled on towards London. Everything felt different now that we were in Britain. A hollow sense of anti-climax blew through our collective heart. What now? We drove through bleak suburbs. Concrete blocks and identical small terraced houses stretched left and right for miles. The bus stopped in front of a grand white building with pillars and steps and 'The Red Cross' neatly engraved on a plaque. The women looked depressed. The reality of our journey suddenly hit home: the Red Cross was all about 'aid', 'disaster', 'war' and 'tragedy'. And we were a product of all those things. This was not a prolonged excursion.

Bluebird

The elegant building, though housing an organization synonymous with all things sad, was far removed from our warring Balkan brutality. When I tried here to imagine anything to do with our war, I could only conjure up images from black and white Second World War films: nurses in dresses and square white head gear; soldiers with bandages, watching the ceiling. That's what I thought might greet us when we entered: we would be ushered into a black and white room with unfolding camp beds and no one would sleep through the grey night.

Instead we found small, knitted flower-patterned blankets on the floor, with more knitted blankets on top, the sum of which formed our beds. Everyone looked around, slightly lost, the middle-class émigrés' dignity melting away like ice-cream down a cone. Some women sat on the floor, children asleep in their arms. Some wandered around the place, trying to look as if they knew what we were supposed to be doing. A Bosnian woman found a cardboard box full of soap and picked up a piece that was shaped like an orange. An English woman saw her and jumped, grabbing the soap from her hand: 'No! Not to eat!' Everyone was aghast: *How dare she, the bitch, doesn't she know we had VCRs and cars and soap bars?* Our English hosts were embarrassed at their colleague's odd behaviour, but we understood the situation: they thought we were savages.

Some of the Bosnian women were desperate to

convince them otherwise. They spent hours explaining that we used to have everything: beds, sheets, extra linen in the cupboards, embroidered, starched; crystal glasses, memories, china, passports, vacuum cleaners, pets, tastes, holidays, smells, sounds, and most of all that we loved, loved each other, that we hadn't spent the last fifty years secretly hating each other's guts, waiting for the first opportunity to rip each other open in the most savage ways. They wanted to explain the war was a mistake, a ploy of evil politicians, it had nothing to do with us, the people sitting before them.

In the meantime I had found a small patch on the floor, amongst the blankets' woolly flowers on the grey office carpet and decided to go to sleep. There was nothing better to do. I was permanently burdened with a ball in my stomach, a burning feeling that pressed my throat. As I was getting ready for bed, I saw one of the English women stepping carefully through the blankets as if the floor were laden with mines. 'There is an extra bed here,' I told her. 'Oh, thank you,' she smiled and settled amongst the flowers. Months later, I lived with this woman and her family in a countryside vicarage, feeling my socialist atheism pulsate while they prayed before each meal. They often prayed for me and my family, for which I was secretly grateful.

Smoking trouble

The next morning we stepped on the bus and drove off, leaving London behind, the only city in Britain we really knew anything about. One by one we took turns under the roof window of the bus and lit up. Cigarette breaks were usually a peaceful time. We watched the sky escape above us and didn't speak if we didn't feel like it, but now our silence was interrupted by a woman who wore tracksuit bottoms with sagging knees and drooping bottom. She leapt up towards us from her seat in a fit of coughing and hollered: 'Extinguish those cigarettes! You are going to kill me! I am a heart patient, I have three pacemakers!' She patted her left breast and produced a symphony of coughing, rich with phlegm and rasping bronchia.

I'd seen this woman before, when we were waiting to board the bus. She was always dressed in the most shabby clothes, and I remember Dragan congratulating her on being the only one who looked like a real refugee. He had said poetically: 'You are the only one reflecting the true tragedy that has gripped our country like a monster's evil claw. You are the only one who can make us look better in these English people's eyes.' And patted her on the nylon shoulder. She was pleased with the praise and had kept up the shabby look fastidiously.

After her anti-smoking barrage, we took hurried, desperate drags and extinguished our cigarettes, with Gordana saying: 'Keep your knickers on, we're off, plenty of fresh air coming your way.' We whispered nervously to each other of the dreaded possibility of a ban on smoking on board for the rest of the trip. We settled back into our warm seats to look yet again at the unfolding asphalt.

'She's that bloody doctor's wife from Sarajevo,' I heard a woman behind me say. 'Yeah, and she's dressed like a tramp. I mean, who is she trying to fool? As if we don't know her and all that she's got,' said another woman. 'Come on,' said another voice, 'if she's a heart patient and we're smoking around her, it's really not right, is it?' Some agreed, others said nothing.

The journey settled back into its sounds of sighing, children's mumbling, and the huffing bus engine catching its breath between shifting gears. I saw a cloud of smoke bloom above an anonymous seat. We waited for the heart patient to unleash her wrath once again, but nothing happened. She was silent. Perhaps she was asleep? I wanted to see who it was that had the courage to smoke in a seat so near hers. Surely they had heard the woman shout not so long ago? Had they no fear?

I approached the curl of smoke with tiny steps, the rest of the bus full of excited expectation at what I might find. I looked over the seat and saw her, the heart patient herself, reclining lopsided, one foot up, one down, spread over two seats. Pacemakers forgotten. She started when she saw me peering at her.

'What's this?' I asked. 'What are you doing? I thought you were dying of heart disease?' I was incredulous. Surely it was some kind of joke.

She laughed feebly, putting the cigarette out. 'I tried to stop,' she said, 'to quit the bloody things.' She sat up, looking guilty. One by one, some of the others came round and when they saw it was she who'd been smoking, invariably yelped in shock and covered their mouths, running back to tell everyone else or waving the rest of the bus over, as if the lady was giving some kind of a show. When the excitement eventually wore off, we lit our cigarettes and puffed upwards into the hole that faced the sky.

The right to fur

It was the final day of our journey, and I slept another uncomfortable, blank sleep. The white light of the sun wrapped in a clingfilm of thin clouds woke me and I blinked, trying to adjust to the brightness. I saw small cottages, greenery, an emerald countryside and felt my heart leap. We had arrived in Kendal. It was beautiful. One part of our group was to stay here, while the rest of us would carry on up to Penrith, our final destination. We were all to take a break here first though.

I saw the pacemaker lady roll out of the bus in her lizard-green shell suit, hair amok, grumpy faced. Gordana was already outside, smoking, a conference around her as usual. The old man who travelled with us to join his daughter in England basked in the occasional ray of sun, his scruffy jumper loose. Esma nervously glanced around, chain smoking. The English were chatting away to the

Kendal hosts, in front of a small church. My sister and I, along with a couple of other girls who spoke some English, were called aside. We were introduced to Brian. He had a white beard that joined his tufty sideburns and made him look as if he was wearing a Santa Claus fake beard. He spoke slowly and loudly, fixing us intently with his eyes: 'WE HAVE SOME CLOTHES INSIDE CHURCH, ALL SORTED FOR EVERYBODY TO LOOK AT AND TAKE WHAT THEY NEED. OR T-SHIRT OR TROUSERS. YES? (intense gaze) CAN YOU PLEASE TELL WOMEN GO IN AND LOOK WHEN NO SMOKE? YES? (nervous smile)' We went from group to smoking group, informing them. Cigarettes were crushed under heels, raising the dust on the gravel.

The church was small and dark. Coloured light peeked through the high stained-glass windows without illuminating the space. The clothes were laid out neatly in a semicircle with a large pile of random items on a long stall in the middle. There were T-shirts of all sizes and lengths, mostly worn out and washed out; trouser legs showed off their patterns; jumpers shone their sequins. Everything smelled of mothballs and plastic. On a separate wall hung fur coats. Brown, white, ochre and glistening black furs. I knew there would be trouble once they were spotted. Too many Slavic women and too few furs.

Within minutes the church became a hive, alive with the noise of fingers working through the second-hand items. Scuffles sounded amongst the cottons and the nylons, and coat hangers made a disapproving noise moving along the metal rail. Temporary chaos filled the House of God when my fur prediction came true. Who was going to get them? Who saw them first? How does charity become the rightful property of a rightful owner?

'I saw it first,' said one.

'So what, I saw it second.'

'I have a small child. I need a fur coat,' said a woman clutching a sleeping child.

'My surname starts with A and that means I am the first on the alphabetical list.'

'What alphabetical list?'

'They have one, the English, go and ask them if you don't believe me.'

Someone went to enquire about the alphabetical list for getting fur coats. The English had no idea what she was talking about. In the meantime, the 'A' woman had stuffed the fur coat into a plastic bag and given it to her daughter to take on the bus. She waited in faux fury for the other woman to come back. The English were brought into the church to rule who would get a fur coat. After hearing all the emotional appeals for the individual rights to fur, they thought about it for a while, with the white-bearded man at their judicial helm looking up at the ceiling as if seeking guidance from God. Finally he announced: 'Because we cannot decide who gets the fur coats, we have decided that no one will get one and we shall take them all back into the charity shops where they will be sold.' The women tried to contest the decision, but that was the final word. The 'A' woman protested too, to cover up the fact that she'd sneaked out the fur in the bag.

The importance of polite words

Only one woman was working away quietly in the Kendal church, giving every item of clothing a good look and a proper feel: Rada, the pacemaker lady. She took her role as refugee very seriously and did everything she thought a real refugee might, such as stockpiling second-hand clothes. She did away with the things she thought a refugee might not care about, like combing her hair or wearing make-up. All the other women applied bright or dark lipstick regularly and fixed their hairdos looking in compact mirrors, but not her. As I stood outside the church, I noticed the English nudge each other and laugh at somebody in the distance. Rada was approaching with a suitcase in one hand and two bin bags in the other. The bags were choking with clothes – sleeves hung out like loose intestines.

There was lunch. Followed by scones and butter.

Then tea. Proper England. They said the region was called 'the Lake District'. I like the Lake District, I thought to myself. As we ate, a group of our English hosts approached me and asked me to interpret. One of them announced: 'In this country, we very much appreciate it if people say "please" when they are asking for something, and respond with a "thank you" when something is given to them.' I translated. 'We have noticed that you Bosnians don't usually say these words, so please can you make an effort from now on?' I translated. The Bosnians said: 'OK' in a surprisingly uninterested way. The old man, who appeared to be enjoying his scones and jam, said: 'Thank you please!' and everyone roared with laughter.

I became so conscious of having to always say 'please' and 'thank you' that months later I found myself saying 'thank you' to an ATM machine, to the general amusement of the people queuing behind me. I imagined them telling their friends and families how a crazy foreign girl, an *Eastern European* – for that is how I was now perceived – was saying thank you to a machine.

The castle

After we left Kendal that afternoon, we were told our homes in Penrith weren't ready yet, and that we'd spend the first few days in a castle in the countryside. We approached it through gardens that seemed to carry on over the hills and into the nearby forest. A grey, white and blue sky was endless above us. We were shown to rooms with four-poster beds and delicate antiques and each of us was amazed that we should end up here, if only for a few days. The beauty of the place finally put an end to the indefatigable bickering about the charity outfits and the odd dispute about someone hoarding all of the castle's toilet paper under their four-poster bed. I took my weighty Walkman and roamed the gardens for hours.

One day I came in from a walk and found Safija, one of the Bosnian women, listing the luxuries of her pre-war home to one of our hosts, who nodded and smiled politely. Safija refused to accept that the English couldn't understand a word of what she was saying. She spoke no English herself. David, a small dark man with a wiry body and a gentle personality, who had come to work with the English volunteers since we'd arrived at the castle, sat down next to Safija. After she had talked to David for some time, asked him questions and received only more smiles and nods, she asked me to translate. I obliged. Safija carried on listing the contents of her home. David was stupefied and I shrugged my shoulders apologetically as I repeated her words in English: '. . . frying pans, jams and pickles, summer and winter carpets, TV, VCR, washing machine, crystal glasses . . .' She recited the items desperately, like a chant, as if trying to conjure up her possessions before her again. Then she said, suddenly: 'You know, David – translate, translate,' she nudged me in the ribs, 'I may not know any English, but perhaps we can communicate in Latin, I am a doctor you know.' I translated. David nodded. 'For example,' she said with a shrewd little smile, 'I know body parts: biceps (which she pronounced as *beeseps*, pointing to David's), triceps (*treeseps*, pinching his arm) and penis (*pehnis*)!' And she pointed a skinny finger at David's crotch. Safija was in fits of laughter. David blushed like an ember. I was in the middle, caught in a joke that needed no translating. Safija had finally conjured up something from home: a bit of Bosnian humour.

Shadows

I had nightmares. One was persistent: empty streets and the clicking of heels. I was hiding, the war was raging and I had nowhere to go. England was only a dream. There was a man, a silver pistol at his hip, a slender man in white tennis shoes, blue jeans and brown T-shirt. I'd never seen him before. He'd say: 'I am the highest authority,' and I'd wake up, sweat burning my face. I'd look at the shadows on the wall, and remember I was in England, that I was a refugee. Relief.

Misfits

The day we left the castle was the day Rada transformed herself into a princess. People were taken one by one or in small groups to have a look at the houses in which they were going to stay. Rada went after breakfast, wearing her usual scruffy attire, although, as I knew by then, she was not a poor woman at all. I didn't see her return, but as I was having a coffee in the hall, she came downstairs wearing an elegant suit with an emerald-coloured coat, matching earrings, her hair styled and calcified with hairspray. Everyone in the hall gasped with surprise. 'What happened to you? We didn't recognize you! Are you not a refugee any more?' the others teased her. 'It was too lovely, the house,' she said, almost hyperventilating with excitement, 'I couldn't go there looking like a rag!' At least Rada tried to do what she thought best. But as with the cigarettes, she always gave in to her nature in the end.

*

Misfits

My sister and I went to see our future home with my future housemate and fellow refugee Nada, and her three-year-old son Sasha. I had been afraid of being put with one of the families and being bossed around by someone else's mother, but Nada was only twenty-eight, and just perfect. She was a little less confused than we were, kind and funny, though I don't envy her having to live with my sister and me, two teenagers. Sasha was sweet and just a little naughty and had taken to speaking gibberish with a fervour – his response to English which was spoken to him and around him, and which he under-stood none of. We were taken to a house at the end of a long street to meet a woman called Eve. There was a barn in her back garden that had been renovated as a home for Eve's daughter, Angie, and Angie was giving up the barn for us.

We were introduced to Eve's six cats, one of them called Fred, who had epileptic fits when Eve vacuumed the floor. Eve seemed to have a thing for adopting the less fortunate. On the first floor of her house lived Philip, a lovely man with Down's syndrome, who, according to Eve, cried when he saw news reports from Bosnia and was happy to hear we were coming to stay in the house. And then there was Margaret, a middle-aged woman who had the mental age of a five-year-old. Both she and Philip were extremely cheerful. When we arrived to see the place there was some commotion going on because

Bluebird

Philip had flushed Margaret's dentures down the toilet. They both thought it was hilarious, but Eve was a bit cross.

I started going to a school on the opposite side of town from where I lived with Nada, Sasha, Eve, Angie, Philip and Margaret, and the six cats. Every morning I was picked up by a boy from school and his father. The boy didn't talk to me much. He just looked a little pissed off that they had to collect me. I would roll into the car still half-asleep and try to mutate into an English speaker on the back seat during the ten-minute ride.

Evenings were spent sitting in pubs with my school mates, trying to understand the fast-paced northern-accented English, as well as drinking cider for the first time in my life and smoking many fags. I soaked up the English language ceaselessly, new words whirring in my head at night when I switched off the light and tried to go to sleep. I pestered my newly acquired friends for the meanings of the words they used, and they insisted I learned to count in old Cumbrian, something I have long since forgotten.

I started saying 'castle' and 'grass' with short northern vowels, until a girl, who became one of my closest friends, took it upon herself to introduce me to what she called 'proper pronunciation'. She instructed me not to say 'luv' but 'lav'; she told me that 'butcher' is 'butcher'

and not 'batcher', as I'd pronounced it, in my vast lin-
guistic confusion. I started attending GCSE English
classes, where we read the poetry of Wilfred Owen. I was
told that many of the pupils feared that I might find the
war imagery too potent, which I found surprising, since I
was still struggling to decipher many of the nouns and
verbs in order to make sense of the images. The class
teacher, Mr Barrett, volunteered to give me private
tutorials to help with my English – I was to write essays
for him, which we would then discuss. We wrote few
essays in Yugoslavia – all our exams were oral – and I
enjoyed the English system of giving the students time
to think, to express themselves, rather than suffer at
the hands of the teachers, who, at least in my school,
relished any opportunity to humiliate the students they
didn't particularly like.

Mr Barrett was kind but unsmiling. One day, after my
first couple of months in Penrith, he remarked on the use
of the word 'like' in my essays. 'Vesna,' he said, '"like" is
a word local people use at the end of every sentence.'
(This was true. The Cumbrians said: 'How's it going, like,
eh?' or 'What's the crack, like, eh?' pretty much all the
time.) 'But,' Mr Barrett said, 'it's not proper English.' He
explained the difference between 'like' and 'as if' and
when I should and shouldn't use them. 'Proper English',
I thought, trying to cram all the information into my head.

I was spared wearing the school uniform because our

estimated time in the UK, that is to say in Penrith, was six months only – everyone had thought that the war would have ended by then and we'd go back home. I wore red jeans and chequered shirts to classes, much to the envy of the rest of the pupils. Initially the teachers attempted to gauge the level of my English by sending me to both A-level and GCSE English classes. The A-level class was studying *Hamlet* and I listened to the incomprehensible words, recognizing only 'Gertrude', 'muther', 'Hamlet', 'Ophelia' and the rest of the names. I'd read *Hamlet* in Serbo-Croat in the term before the outbreak of war, but it didn't help me decipher the original. I sat and listened quietly for weeks, without any participation in class discussions. When my classmates started reading William Blake, I longed to understand. I decided to volunteer a comment when we studied *The Sick Rose*. I spoke briefly, mentioning death and love. A vast silence spread across the classroom, with everyone – teacher and students – staring at me. I couldn't work out if what I had said was nonsense or whether it was the sheer shock of hearing me speak after I'd been taciturn for weeks that sent everyone into gawping speechlessness.

On Friday and Saturday nights the school crowd went to Penrith Pride, an old worn-out pub with tumbledown seats and a thinning mucus-green carpet. The owner, her husband and their dog hosted bad rock gigs and let us drink as much cheap cider as we liked. On Monday mornings the boys listed the number of pints they had 'downed' over the weekend. I was fascinated by their pride and fierce competition at who remembered least from the evening. Back home, drinking wasn't so popular – we'd smoke one joint between five of us and be stoned for the entire week. The first time I'd ever been drunk was on New Year's Eve of 1992.

I missed light, and was soaked with rain and beaten by northern winds. I took photography classes at school and took pictures of fields, trying to capture rain rushing diagonally across the horizon or drizzling feebly on to the grass. I hid in the darkroom, developing prints for hours on end.

Jude

My sister moped around for the two months she managed to stick it out in Penrith. She hadn't completed her schooling in Bosnia, but she was too old for school and no one could decide what she should do next. She'd left her boyfriend of six months back in Croatia, a raven-haired twenty-something-year-old, and they pined away for each other in letters and very expensive phone calls. My mother, who had little faith in teenage love affairs and was afraid of what would come of me if I were left alone, tried to dissuade her from leaving England, but, as everyone knows, teenage love can break most bonds, let alone simple asylum claims. My sister decided to return to Croatia in December 1992, and I waved goodbye to her from Penrith's small train station with Jude.

I had met Jude at Safeway, the town's biggest supermarket. He worked at the checkout. I went there to see my first big supermarket and got blown away by the choice of margarine. We had only one type of margarine back home, called Dobro Jutro! (Good Morning!), with a jolly-looking cow, smiling at the breakfaster, but here I was, staring at olive oil-infused margarine, margarine that couldn't believe it wasn't butter, margarine that was fat-free, semi-fat and very fat.

I tried to pick out a hair colour. I wanted red, but there were so many reds, all offering great things. I couldn't buy any for fear of making the wrong choice. So I picked up a pint of milk and headed for the checkout, and as I queued I saw Jude in a white uniform, dropping the groceries all over the place, in front of irritated customers. He was smiling at his own clumsiness and I felt an affinity with him immediately. So I went to Safeway a lot and always queued at his till, my heart jumping as he dropped and bruised my fruit and vegetables, and smashed my tomatoes. Then one day he asked me if I would meet him for a drink after work.

Out of his supermarket uniform, Jude wore an over-sized coat, a pair of tatty old boots, voluminous trousers and a ruffled shirt, and smoked roll-ups that came out in various shapes: pear, banana, cucumber. They never stayed lit, always crumbling and burning holes in his clothes. He fell over everything. He would walk into a pub and, on his way to say hello to a group of friends, trip over at least three chairs. I fell in love deeply.

I felt normal for the first time in months. Jude didn't ask me about dead people, about devastation, didn't display any of the morbid curiosity that so many people did. He asked about me as if I were a normal girl from Penrith. We talked music, the Cure, Neil Young, Tim Buckley. We sang songs in the dark wet night, the pallid street lights occasionally showing glints of teeth in a smile. We listened to music and read books. Sometimes we argued and then I wouldn't pick him up after work outside Safeway. And in December I went to spend Christmas with him and his family in the countryside.

His home was a cottage sitting alone in a white snowy field with a frozen lake nearby. The basement was stacked with his father's paintings; one of them showed Margaret Thatcher's face in a broken mirror. His father was a kind, bearded man, just how you would expect a country artist to look, and his mother had hair down to her waist and spoke in a soft voice. That Christmas I forgot who I was, why I was there; I forgot that there was a war, that people were dying, that I had no family around me, that I knew nobody. After lunch we all relaxed in our bedrooms, I with Jude on the bunk bed in his room that wasn't really a room, but more like a train compartment with a poster of Marilyn Monroe pouting a gentle kiss at us. Jude's father took us for a walk in the afternoon, just as the sky was changing from electric blue to indigo. We went to the lake, which had apparently not frozen over for years until that day. Our hot cheeks burning in the cold air.

The accountant

Wednesday was the day we received our Income Support. When my sister left, I was given my own booklet with which I walked to the post office every Wednesday. This day was greeted with joy and everyone came to the Quaker Meeting House after collecting their pennies to give part of their money towards the Return Fund the organizers had set up to collect money for our return tickets once our six months in the UK had expired.

The accountant looked like something from an old photograph, in tailored tweed suits and small pebble glasses. He wrote in cramped movements, tiny numbers crowding the pages. He had everyone's name carefully written out and added their contribution next to it. I received £23.75 weekly and after I gave him my £7 donation I had £16.75. I would then walk uphill to our house while black clouds of birds whooshed above, and give

The accountant

Nada £10 for our weekly food shopping. Finally I was left with £6.75 for the week. I bought a packet of Silk Cut and had £4.75. Then, at the petrol station, I would buy three chocolate bars and eat them ravenously at the bench opposite, by the road, at sunset. I was left with £3.75. I can't remember what I did with that.

Wednesday after Wednesday we queued in front of the accountant's desk at the Quaker Meeting House. Afterwards we sat around the long tables in the main room discussing our immigration issues with each other, and the impossibility of finding preserved vine leaves or decent olive oil in England. As weeks went by, the subject of why the Return Fund had been set up in the first place was raised with ever greater ferocity. Gordana was particularly vocal about this and the other women were happy to back her up. One day she took a piece of paper and a calculator and worked out the numbers: how long have we been here? Three months. How many weeks is that? Twelve and something. Right. How many women? Twenty-five. How much do they receive each week? Thirty-five pounds.

Gordana held the pen by its little throat as if it were the accountant himself. The result of her calculations was awaited with tension. The tip of her pink tongue stuck out at the corner of her mouth, pointing upwards. Finally, a figure shot through her purple lips like a death sentence. *Aaahs* of shock came out of the many mothers' mouths, *tsttsts* sounded as their tongues clicked against their teeth. Anger rose visibly, as in cartoons, when faces redden from the bottom up. The women spoke in whispers about what to do and soon a mutiny broke out. The accountant's little desk was stormed and questions were thrown at him like Molotov cocktails.

'Why are you taking our money away when we are already receiving so little?' asked Gordana.

The accountant looked bewildered.

'What are we getting in return?'

The accountant started to sweat.

'Give us all that money back!'

'I'm afraid it's not up to me . . . I'm just here to . . .'

'Who is it up to?' Gordana spat the words like fire. Her buttocks were firm in the purple leggings. She stood with her hands on her hips, the black plait threatening as if it were a whip she always carried around. Rada sat elegantly on the side, watching the battle.

'What's going on here?'

It was M. She had entered the room.

M was a stern woman, tall and slim, in slacks and comfortable leather shoes. She was one of the top people in the organization, though she wasn't among those who had gone to Croatia to collect us, and feelings about her were mixed. Some thought she was 'a real lady, like Princess Diana', others found her 'steely, like Margaret Thatcher'.

When M walked into the room and said: 'What's going

on here?' the accountant's relief was palpable. It was as if someone had just cut him loose from a rope. He started gathering his papers maniacally.

'Not so fast, Mr accountant,' growled Gordana, slapping her palm on the bunch of papers he had just scavenged, without turning around to look at him. She was facing M.

M was considered 'a lady of authority' in the local circles and the automatic assumption was that she would hold the same status among the Bosnian women. But the Bosnian contingent had no interest in M: Gordana was the queen bee in this hive. She looked at M, put a cigarette between her lips and clicked her fingers for a lighter. The other women circled around them and Rada got up to light Gordana's cigarette. She was beaming with delight at taking part in the scene.

'There's no smoking here,' M said icily.

'Says who?' asked Gordana, chewing her gum like a gangster, taking a deep drag of her cigarette and exhaling voluptuous clouds of smoke into the room.

'It's the rules Gordana, you know it as well as I do. The Quakers don't like it.'

'Oh yeah? Well, now there is. The Quakers *and you* can kiss my arse.'

She started taking wide slow steps towards M. Her thighs were clutched, each muscle like a rock, no cellulite, no shivering of fatty flesh. She stopped one step in front of M, took another drag on her cigarette, and blew the smoke straight into her face. I thought I was watching a film. M tried to remain composed, but coughed and moved a step back despite herself, her cool crushed with a single puff of smoke.

'Why are you taking our money?'

'Because we are collecting a fund for you, to make sure . . .'

'It is bull*shit*!' Gordana said and I was sure she'd been watching Westerns all her life, preparing for a standoff like this one. 'Now tell me, really, why are you taking our money?' She looked fierce. I wouldn't have liked to have been M in that moment.

'Gordana, if you don't believe me, you can ask Brian.'

'I want *you* to tell me, you are boss around here, it seems. You come into the room and say "What's going on?" This is what's going on: give back our money. Boss.' Another puff of smoke in the face.

Gordana was delivering a first-class act. M turned on her heel, stifled a cough and walked out into the other room. Everyone whooped and applauded, for M's exit meant victory for Gordana. Gordana smiled, put her cigarette out and sat down. 'We'll see now who's boss. Taking away our money like that . . .'

After that there was another gathering at the Quaker Meeting House. I translated. The English explained that the money was for the return tickets, the Bosnians booed, the English attempted to discuss, the Bosnians jeered and started chanting 'Give us back our money' as if a performance they'd paid for had been cancelled or proved highly disappointing. After some more exasperating attempts at a democratic solution, which the Bosnians invariably boycotted, the money was handed back. Gordana supervised the calculations with the accountant, who was sweating beside her. She teased him: 'Mr, you so nervous! Like you never sit next to woman before!' And the accountant blushed like an over-ripe peach. He stared so hard at the piece of paper next to him that I thought he would get eye cramp.

'When we finish calculations, we go and celebrate with champagne!' she said and gave him a little wink.

A letter from my father

I developed a morning ritual in those first months in Britain: get up, put the kettle on, run across the cold yard into Eve's kitchen to see if any letters have arrived. The Royal Mail had become my lifeline. Correspondence came from all over the world: Norway, Sweden, the US, Holland, from all the friends who had escaped like me to any country that would have them. Nada expected letters from her father and husband who wrote weekly. Sometimes it would take a while for the letters to arrive and then the front door would vomit them all together on to Eve's carpet. Those days were a feast. Philip would stack them neatly on the kitchen table for me to collect.

Nada would be preparing coffee and Sasha eating his little breakfast when I came in with the post for both of us, rubbing my cold hands as I closed the front door. We sat down around our steaming cups of coffee, the sun shedding optimism into the room, and picked out the envelopes bearing our names. On one of them, to my surprise, my father's familiar, angular writing had carefully spelled the English address in large letters.

My father was in Bosnia, refusing to leave, his alcoholism steep like a trench. His father was also a drinker, as was my uncle. My grandfather died long before I was born, and I never knew much about him, apart from that he was buried in Belgrade, miles away from home. I remember the trees and the silence when I visited his grave at the age of six, with my mother. My grandmother was a kind woman, who wore chiffon dresses and had a large fig tree outside her house. I never knew how she dealt with having an alcoholic husband and sons (though there were three other alcohol-free children too). She died early enough to be spared seeing her sons, two grown men, drunk to the point where they ceased to be recognizable as themselves. My uncle idolized my father and drank to keep up with him at first, until his own habit became cemented. He was kind and willowy, a benign presence who once made a pass at my mother in his boozed-up oblivion; I watched him put his hand on her knee, beneath our dining table. My mother, shocked, brushed it off so that no one noticed, and he placed his elbows on the table, his hands where everyone could see them, embarrassed. It was like a scene from a film about problem families, where values declined with dwindling self-worth, which is partly what was going on in our home. From then on, whenever my uncle came round I felt a mixture of affection and repulsion towards him, though no one suspected my feelings.

My father drank for most of my life. My mother met him when he was on the wagon – he'd made a bet with a friend that he could do without drinking for six months, a bet that, had my mother been older than her twenty-one years, would have probably alarmed her in itself. They talked and strolled through Mostar's streets, per-fumed with linden flowers in summer and quilted with plane-tree leaves in autumn, my father's geeky side emerging when he brought mathematical problems for them to try to solve together. When the bet was won he started drinking again, but as he was a young man in his early twenties his excessive drinking was not considered serious. Alcoholics in my town were generally referred to as men who 'like to have a drink', even as their marriages collapsed, their careers failed, their piss-soaked bodies rotted and had to be collected by their long-suffering friends or family members from various cheap bars in town. Booze was a part of local life as much as alfresco dining in the summer or year-round afternoon walks.

My parents married a year after their first date. Their wedding photo shows a handsome couple surrounded by their families, Serbs on my father's side, Croats on my mother's. Herzegovina's Serbs live largely in the eastern part, while the Croats are in the west, and despite their inhabiting a relatively small region, the saying 'ne'er the twain shall meet' thoroughly captures the spirit of the two peoples' relationship. It is reported that, during the Second World War, Herzegovina's Croats killed Herzegovina's Serbs with such fervour that even the Germans and Italians, who backed their hatred, didn't know how to stop them. In turn, the Serbs pummelled the Croats and Muslims in the 1990s, with equal ferocity.

It is said that my father's announcement back in the early 1970s that he planned to marry a girl from western Herzegovina wasn't met with universal joy, though everyone was polite when my mother was introduced to the family. On my mother's side, no one minded much. When Socialist Yugoslavia was formed, my grandmother hung a picture of Tito next to her favourite crucifix on the wall, the smiling atheist Marshal radiant next to a bloodied Jesus. My mother's family's single-nationality seal had been broken years earlier, when my auntie, some ten years my mother's senior, brought her Muslim lover to their native village and introduced him as 'Stjepan from Sarajevo'. They'd agreed that he'd pose as a Croat until everyone met him and grew to love him, and that they'd reveal his real identity afterwards, when his non-Christianity would be irrelevant given his wonderful personality. Their plan was blown on the second day, however, when someone recognized my future uncle and said: 'Hey Mustafa! What are you doing in these parts?' in front of everyone. Fortunately, the family already liked him, and my aunt and uncle went on to share more than thirty years of marriage.

My mother said that my father drank when my sister was born and carried on drinking into her infancy and that, had he not gone to a rehab clinic and dried up two years later, I would never have been born. Five months into her pregnancy with me, my mother's waters were at the point of breaking, and our family doctor ordered her to spend the remaining four months in bed. It's not only life that's an uncertainty, conception and gestation are too; one can never relax. My father was sober for six years after that, and those were 'the golden years' of my parents' marriage, according to my mother. During this time I formed a strong bond with my father; at my insistence, he told me stories from his childhood before I went to sleep (most of which featured accounts of diving off Mostar's Old Bridge for cigarettes at sixteen); he supervised my sister's and my somersault attempts, bought a yoga exercise book and tried to heal my mother's headaches with bio-energy (which, by the way, didn't work). In an attempt to cool down our small, hot flat that turned into a boiling blister in the 40°-plus summer temperatures, he built a primitive version of an air-conditioning unit that consisted of a wet cloth attached to a fan (it was partially effective). He per-formed silly jokes for all of us, we invented a new language that was based on Serbo-Croat words but with entirely new meanings, and he designed and built an awning for our sun-scorched balcony that shaded us for decades. When he fell off the wagon for the last time, the thud was deafening.

His engineering career had been going well, and he was offered a six-month project in Russia. He went away for four months but returned early. My mother and I were returning from an evening stroll – I was six years old at the time – and we found my father asleep outside the front door. A furious smell of vodka emanated from his mouth, cavernous and snoring. A few months later, on his way back from a wedding party, my father met the eighteen-year-old daughter of a friend and offered her a lift home. Driving into Mostar, he fell asleep behind the wheel, left the road and smashed into a rock. The friend's daughter died on the spot and my father broke his shoulder; the fracture healed but ached for the rest of his life at the slightest weather change, ramming back a moment he could never forget.

The girl's family came to our home every day after the accident for an entire month, crying and mourning in our living room, as if that might somehow alleviate their grief. During their visits, my father hid in his room or went out, unsuccessfully trying to duck his guilt; my mother sat with the mourning parents, helpless and beaten by the accusation they radiated. After that month, the family pressed charges against my father, and he served a year's prison sentence in Mostar's penitentiary.

My sister and I were ignorant of all this – we were told our father had gone away on business, and that he would be back in a year. I wrote him postcards, in which I asked him to bring me three things I wished for most throughout my childhood: a typewriter, a camera and a monkey. I was obsessed with the sound of the typewriter, I wanted to take photos, and I yearned to have a pet that would hug me twenty-four hours a day. My mother took my postcards to my father, down the road, to the prison.

When he came out, the dead girl's parents returned to our living room, bringing back a nightmare my parents thought they might start trying to recover from; it was only after my father's eldest sister came over and told them that they must go home and leave my parents alone, that they stopped coming round. The story was taboo in our house and I found out about it only after the war started, my mother blurting out that my father had been to jail, her caution lowered by the gravity of our lives at the time. I found it hard to imagine the enormity of my father's guilt, shame and, perhaps, self-loathing, things that we never had a chance to talk about, and that I would never have been able to understand at that age. After he came out of prison, our family's daily life revolved, to a lesser or greater degree, on my father's drunken behaviour: the contrast between him sober

A letter from my father

(when he was kind, funny and generous) and drunk (when he was aggressive, insecure and volatile), and the debts he incurred after spending all his money on drink.

Sometimes he would be delivered like a giant parcel with a great clunk of his collapsing body on the doorstep.

And since the war began, his drinking had got worse, ending only when he was unconscious. My mother said that he and the neighbours brewed their own booze by mixing 100 per cent alcohol with a couple of stems of herbs, to add flavour, apparently. I always wondered why they cared about flavour when they drank anything that would inebriate. They would apparently get so drunk that they were unable to go to the shelters when the general warnings sounded. One of their many ploys to get hold of a drink was to take turns going to a place where they sold local brandy, but which was quite far away, so you had to go either by car or on a bicycle. When my father's turn came, he rode our kiddie bicycle there. This time, on his way back he drove into a ditch and broke his leg. He was hospitalized, and therefore sober, and my mother brought him the letters I had written over the months. That's when he started writing to me. These letters remain my only real insight into my father's mind.

My dear daughter,
How are you? How is England treating you?
Your mother tells me you are homesick. Please,

don't be a fool. Here, life is madness, shells are falling every day, they are destroying everything. What would you do here? The other day I helped carry five boys from our yard into the hospital. They were playing outside when a shell hit and injured them all. Do you want to see things like that? I would get out of here if I could, but I can't. Who's going to put up with a fool like me? There is nowhere for me to go.

I went to see Mr Bosko the other day, you remember him? The painter from our neighbourhood? Well, he's struggling to work these days, says there's nothing left to paint. He was helping out at the hospital at first and not painting at all. But then he said he started having nightmares and had to paint the dead and the wounded. They were magnificent paintings. Old Bosko is a great artist. Then he stopped. He couldn't go to the hospital any more, said he couldn't handle it, and tried to go to the countryside and paint some landscapes, to calm himself, remind himself of harmony. I even went with him one day, but they stopped us, the army, and sent us back, said there was an 'action' going on, it was dangerous. So now he has a blank canvas hanging on his living-room wall, like a cloud, I tell him. He says that it might inspire him, tell him what to paint. When I went to see him, we sat around talking and looking at the blank canvas.

Recently, there has been some unrest between the Croats and the Muslims too. That's bad. There are stories of concentration camps. Strange how far away in time the Second World War seems, yet here we are, doing all the same beastly things. The city is already divided. Uncle Hojica has his house in the old town and he's asking if he can come and stay with me here. His house has been taken over by his relatives, they ran from the army who burnt down their houses in a neighbouring village. They say there is rape, slaughter, thieving.

I get food from Caritas. They give us food in bags, you remember, we all ate it together, the liquid chicken packs and the salty feta cheese. I don't like going there much, because everyone fights all the time. You really have to shove people to get your bit of chicken.

You are living a normal life there, kids your age here aren't even going to school any more. Everyone's just sitting in the shelters all day long.

Be good my darling and don't be homesick.

Alisa

I came back from school, hung up my coat and threw my keys on the kitchen table. They landed with a crash, knocking a letter to the floor. I picked it up off the carpet and saw Arabic writing stretched across the stamp and below in the Latin alphabet: 'United Arab Emirates'. I ripped the soft paper of the envelope and read:

Dear Vesna,

Look where I'm writing from! The Arab Emirates! You must be thinking 'What is she doing there?' and you're right. I am still reeling from all the things that have gone on in the last few months, but at least now I'm here.

About a month and a half ago, trouble started between the Muslims and the Croats. They said all Muslims had to leave the city and started taking people out of their buildings, making them stand in a line and arresting them. They arrested my parents and me too, even though my mother is Serb. Women don't matter anyway, do they? Thank God my sister was in Croatia at the time. Anyway, they took us to the airport, to the hangars. They separated men and women and children too. I was alone and I could see my parents looking for me, in a panic. I was so scared. I was never so scared in my life. They came up to us, searched us. They slapped people if they asked questions. We were called horrible names all the time.

Then some big fat sergeant came to inspect us. It was hot, the sun was beating like a hammer, and we had to stand in the middle of the airport field. He looked around and ordered that only the men be kept, the women and children had to go. 'We'll look bad in front of the International Community if we keep the women and children.' They all laughed and let us go. My mother grabbed me and led me out. She was crying, and I was looking for my father, who was led into some room at the airport. I was shouting for my father, but my mother was pulling me away and I saw some kids being hit with guns for trying to run to their fathers. So I shut up and looked at my shoes and I walked and walked and we had to walk all the way back into the city, the shells smashing the pavement like hammers.

Bluebird

My father is still there. My mother sent me here with a family friend who had something organized through some charity. It is a Muslim charity and I have to go to the mosque. I've never been religious, but I am starting to find solace in prayer. I pray for my father all the time, hoping he'll be fine.

It's strange here, but I am happy that I don't have to be in Mostar any more. I saw your mother before I left, and she said that you are homesick. Don't be. It's hell there.

Write to me, I miss you very much and our times together at school.

Kisses,

Alisa

Alisa was one of the last friends I saw before leaving Mostar. We'd met during a break in attacks and smoked illicitly behind the bar where we used to hang out in pre-war days, but which now stood deserted and cold. She had stayed behind after I left, thinking, like many, that the war would be over before we knew it.

Joni and Jehovah

'Hi, I'm Joni and I'm a Jehovah's witness.' She stood outside the door, hand extended for a shake, red-haired and smiling. I'd just been watching *A Streetcar Named Desire* and was under the spell of Brando's black-and-white handsomeness and Vivien Leigh's contagious melodrama. Nada and Sasha had gone away for a week to London, to visit some long-lost cousins. I was enjoying the time on my own and didn't want anyone knocking on my door, but I'd opened it anyway.

'Hi.' I looked her up and down. 'You go to my school, right?'

She frowned and said: 'I don't recognize you.'

'Oh,' I said. 'So, what do you sell?' I looked at a bunch of books and magazines in her arms and read upside down: '*The Watchtower*. Is that a music magazine?'

'No,' she said, looking at me in disbelief. 'I'm a

Jehovah's Witness.' She enunciated the last words clearly.

'What's that?'

'Well, it's a religion. There are many benefits to joining Jehovah's Witnesses. Would you like to know more?'

I let her in. She put her books and magazines on the table. She looked tired.

'Have you been to many people's doors today?'

'Yes. I went around this whole neighbourhood.'

I made coffee and we sat down to talk. She told me things about Jehovah's Witnesses and I listened. It sounded nuts.

'I am not interested in your religion, I am sorry.' I tried to sound as polite as possible. 'You see I am an atheist. I don't like religion. It just causes trouble in the world.'

She said she understood but didn't leave. Instead, we talked about school and the people there, about Penrith and boys. We agreed that Marlon Brando was the most handsome actor ever. Apart from maybe Johnny Depp, but in a different way. Then I asked her if she'd ever seen *A Streetcar Named Desire* and she said no, that her parents didn't let her watch films that are not about God. In fact, she said, her parents didn't let her do any-thing much outside the group's socializing and her flute playing, so we sat on the sofa, drank tea and melted at Brando's masculine broodiness for the rest of the afternoon.

Joni and Jehovah

Joni was beautiful and smart. Her red hair was straight and long, always pulled back into a modest pony-tail. She grinned a wide, watermelon-slice smile. We became friends. At school we would meet for coffee and watch the small world of Penrith go by. Sometimes we ate lunch at the local pub. Sometimes we escaped into the darknes of the cinema, or cycled across hazy, damp fields. She took me to her house once and introduced me to her parents, who looked like characters in a Victorian painting, stiff and unsmiling. Joni played me something on her flute to hide her embarrassment. I watched her lips curl over the mouthpiece and she taught me to make a sound, blowing downwards.

We laughed and shouted, and my feeble attempts on the flute resounded through the house. Her stern mother appeared in the doorway, her chignon firm, not a loose hair streaking into the halo of the backlight. I fell silent as I saw her feet stomping the wooden clog soles on the floorboards. Joni stopped playing and looked at her mother with a pair of scared doggy eyes. I'd never seen her scared doggy eyes before. Her eyes were usually bright, vivacious, intelligent; these eyes were whimpering and obedient. These must be Jehovah's Witness's eyes, I thought. Frightened of the end of the world. Of Judgement Day.

'Joni, it's going to be supper time soon. Why don't you and your friend finish what you're doing and you can come down and help me with setting the table.' Her voice was bell-like, bouncing on the walls, its snubbing tone poking me out of the room.

'All right mother,' Joni said in her Jehovah's Witness voice.

With Joni's family I had a silent lunch, occasionally punctured by her father's questions about Bosnia and how I liked Penrith. He also asked me about my religion, and when Joni said: 'Dad!', he gave her a look out of the side of his eyes that could have cut a loaf of bread in half. I told him the same thing I'd said to Joni: that I was an atheist and that religion was trouble. He said: 'Mhm,' and tucked into his dinner, changing the subject back to school.

I was never invited to their house again. After that day, Joni's brother checked on her during our lunch hour, which meant that we couldn't meet as we had done before. He went with her to her 'house calls' so she couldn't come to my house and watch videos and drink tea on the sofa. I was sad.

Then Joni's parents announced they had to go away for a few weeks and had decided to leave Joni and her brother behind. This was unprecedented and never likely to happen again. Joni was ecstatic. The day before they left, she ran towards me in the common room.

'They are leaving for two weeks!' she said excitedly.

'Wow! And they're leaving you alone? What about your brother, is he staying?'

'Yes, but I'll get rid of him. We have to go to the pub. I want to drink beer and smoke cigarettes. Tell your friend Paulie – you know the one you said fancied me? – tell him to come to the pub too. I want to kiss a man. I want to sleep with a man. It's now or never.'

I was worried. Our illicit friendship had just shifted into fifth gear and I had been promoted from simply a regular, though disapproved of, 'friend' to a 'provider-of-sin friend' for a Joni dying to go off the rails for two weeks. Had her parents been hedonists instead of Jehovah's Witnesses, she would have made them proud. We went to the pub, drank Guinness and smoked. Joni held her cigarettes clumsily and blew thick clouds of smoke out of the side of her mouth. Paulie was employed, to his delight, to introduce Joni to the world of carnal pleasures.

Her brother, whose ever-present gaze followed her, caught her sneaking out of Paulie's house, ruffled and sexed-out at three o'clock in the morning. There was a scene, Paulie reported – a quiet one apparently. Joni's just-out-of-bed hair was pointed to several times by her brother, who then took her by the arm and led her home, disappearing amongst the heavy oaks that lined the street. And then she vanished for the whole summer.

She didn't come to school for the first week of the new term, and when she did turn up it was only so that the teacher could announce it was her last day there. She was changing schools. She didn't speak to me but only waved as she left. I didn't insist on trying to talk to her. I had no idea what kind of surveillance she was under now and didn't want to get her in even more trouble. Afterwards I called her house several times, but her parents always said she was 'unavailable'. Once I even tried to go to her new school, to sneak a chat, but I saw her brother standing outside in the yard, a bodyguard in the making.

One day Paulie said he saw her going to school from his window. 'Did she look up?' I asked him, checking out his new records.

'She did, but that moron of a brother said something and she lowered her head. What a pity . . . She was a fun girl. We could have had something,' said Paulie, cigarette smoke whirling around his face. He looked like a gumshoe brooding over a broad, like a melancholy Brando, though not as brutish or handsome. I felt like watching *Streetcar*.

Instead, I put a Neil Young record on the small metal nipple of the turntable and landed the needle on the smooth black piste that leads to the first song. We sat back to listen to the music escaping through the half-opened window.

Independence

After six months of living with Nada and Sasha, Nada's husband arrived and I had to move out. Emma, an English woman who was married to a vicar and was part of the convoy, invited me to live with her family. She said that everyone had agreed that I was too young to be on my own and needed support. I had taken to the pint-counting partying habits of my school friends and a typical teenage lifestyle was apparently alarming when embraced by a young foreign girl on her own. I was nettled by the idea that I had been discussed as some-one who couldn't take care of herself, and I was defiant: I didn't need looking after. I was – I liked this word – independent.

With the help of one of the Penrith volunteers, I looked for a house share. We saw a few places and finally settled on a lovely attic room in a large Victorian house.

Bluebird

Three men lived there, but I was to share the downstairs kitchen and bathroom with only one of them – there was another kitchen and bathroom for the others on the first floor. I moved my two suitcases in – one containing clothes and the other books I'd lugged from Bosnia – and a few days later I decided to invite friends over for a housewarming party. Four people turned up. When I went to the kitchen to get some of the drinks chilling in the fridge, I met the housemate who shared the kitchen and bathroom with me. 'I'm Mike,' he said and put out a limp hand. He was skinny, wore disconcertingly tight jeans, had long greasy hair and a thick Scottish accent. He said something about the washing machine, but I didn't understand him. It was my first encounter with a Scottish accent, and I'd only just about mastered comprehension of the northern one. I smiled a lot and nodded, and invited him in for drinks with my four friends. He said something I didn't get and I went back upstairs. Half an hour later, he came into the room bearing a bottle of beer that he claimed was very expensive and special.

He spoke to a few of the people there and announced that the reason one of the housemates didn't want to say hello to me – something I'd noticed but had said nothing about – was because he felt sorry for me. He stared at me when he spoke. 'You're a refugee, you see,' he said, as if that was enough explanation. He then became slightly hostile to Paulie, one of my closest friends at the time, on the bizarre and incorrect assumption that Paulie was 'on benefits'. Around one in the morning my friends went home. Mike stayed, sitting on the chair in the middle of the room. I had nothing more to say to him and I was getting tired, so I pretended I was hungry. That would at least get him out of my room, I thought. He followed me to the kitchen and watched me eat a fried egg. 'You eat very elegantly,' he said and I was flushed with repulsion – I didn't want him to observe me with even a suggestion of sensuality. I started to regret moving into the house. I doubted my independence instantly and intensely.

He invited me to have a look at his CDs, which I accepted reluctantly, afraid of offending him. I'd seen many films featuring psychos who bore much resemblance to Mike. It was 1.30 a.m. and none of the other housemates was around. Mike's room was covered in 1980s black and white posters of women in colour-highlighted underwear, reclining on large motorbikes. I was relieved by this because his preference was obviously for busty, curvaceous women and I was very skinny and flat-chested. It was probably the first time I was grateful for my boyish physique. Mike was keen for me to name a song I liked in his CD collection. I picked one at random and said I needed to go to bed. He didn't offer to go with me.

On my way up the stairs a woman appeared, claiming

that her golden earrings were missing. She was apparently the girlfriend of Andy, the man who lived in the room next to mine and whom I'd not yet met. 'I keep telling him to get a fucking lock on the door, man, but he won't listen to me, will he, like?' I wanted to go to bed but had to stand and listen to her. Mike came up the stairs, delighted that he might inflict his company on someone. He listened to the girl's rant silently and suddenly said that Paulie, my friend, must have stolen the earrings.

'What?' I was incredulous.

'It must have been him, it couldn't have been anyone else,' he said. 'He must have gone into Andy's room when we weren't watching.'

'Bullshit!' Suddenly I wasn't afraid of Mike any longer. I was angry.

'No, it was Paulie,' he insisted. 'He stole the earrings. Let's go to his house. Sort this out face to face.'

It was already past 2 a.m. Anyway, I wasn't worried because Paulie was much bigger than Mike and would have been amused by the situation. 'OK, let's go,' I said.

Andy's girlfriend said she'd have another look round the room, just in case. We waited. I didn't speak, and Mike paced up and down the corridor. Finally, the woman appeared with the golden hoops in her hand. 'They were under Andy's pillow. He sometimes hides my jewellery when he goes away. He's afraid I'll get tarted up and go out, you see.'

I went to my room, angry and afraid again, bolted the door and put a chair under the handle, like in the movies. I went to bed. I wanted my mother.

I woke up the next morning to Mike banging on the wall of his room (which was directly underneath mine). He was playing the song I'd chosen the night before, at full volume. I got dressed quickly and went to Paulie's house, telling him how he was nearly accosted under suspicion of being a jewellery thief. 'You should have let him come, I would have shown him my ice pick,' he said. I laughed, envying his fearlessness. I stayed at Paulie's for at least a week after that, uneasy about going back to the house. When I did return, my room was cold and lonely, empty and unlived in. I missed having someone to talk to at home, I missed eating with people. It was only there that I spent time unbuffered by school and daily activities. And it was there that I understood the potency of loneliness.

My friend Suzy, my informal received pronunciation teacher, came over a couple of times and I prepared mountains of mashed potatoes for us. I had no idea that quantities mattered in cooking. I went to buy a bra – I owned only one, from the church in Kendal – at Marks & Spencer, picking one up and paying for it without looking at the size. I had no idea what size I was and it never occurred to me that I might get the wrong one. My mother had bought things for me before and I had never paid attention. Luckily – perhaps it was a case of trivial divine intervention – the bra fitted fine. I stayed over at Suzy's house for weeks (when I wasn't staying at Paulie's), taking comfort and refuge in the warmth of anyone else's family, until I decided it was time to eat some humble pie and call Emma to see if the offer of her home was still open.

I moved to their house and lived in a partitioned room, off the kids' bedroom. The house was ten miles outside Penrith, attached to a vicarage. The family had four children, two little ones and two teenagers. One of them, Dominic, was my age and went to school with me. Dominic and I played music in their garage, went out drinking in Penrith Pride and set off smoke alarms in his bedroom late at night. I was able to rebel again, my courage and character restored by the backdrop of family life. We took their funny mongrel dog for long walks in the surrounding fields. I cycled to and from Penrith, and loved the nature that filled every corner of the horizon.

When I went to collect my things from the house, Mike entered my room and stood by the door. He came in silently and I glimpsed his skinny legs but pretended I hadn't seen him. 'You're moving out,' he said. I nodded and collected my drawing pencils and put them into one of the two suitcases. 'I found my mother,' he said. I looked up at him. It was perhaps only the second or third time we had ever spoken, but the suggestion of the troubled, intense loneliness that he carried frightened me. 'I was adopted,' he said. 'And now I've found my mother. I am going to meet her. I was wondering if you would come with me?' I thanked God – the one that my temporary family worshipped on Sundays at church and every day before meals – that I'd made the decision to move out. I smiled at Mike and said: 'Thank you. I can't now, but next time, perhaps. Good luck, anyway.' He nodded and moved out of the way as I took my two cases down the stairs. I understood that, just like me, Mike wanted to have a family, to belong, even if temporarily. And I felt that he'd perhaps sniffed out the loneliness in me, that it had made him think we were kindred spirits. The idea made me shudder.

As I left the house I saw Andy, the DJ, driving past in his brown car, windows rolled down, techno blasting. That's what he liked to do, apparently, drive around town with the music turned all the way up, drowning everything else out.

A testimony

As my English gradually improved, I started translating for ex-Yugoslavs when the occasional new arrival needed to make a statement at the makeshift immigration office in the Lake District. On my first day, I arrived at the cement immigration building, reported to the reception desk and sat on a wooden bench. I watched the man sitting opposite me, his hair grey and his cheeks sallow. A woman appeared and called us both into a room. Three immigration officers sat next to one another, their tape recorders ready and pens pressed against their notebooks. We sat down and I translated.

'My name is A. H. I am a primary school teacher from Mostar. I was arrested two months ago. Some men, soldiers, knocked on my door and asked me for my papers. When I brought them out, they ripped everything up and told me to go with them. I don't know who these people were, but I hope that I will find them one day. I went with them and they took me to a cellar of a building by the front line, the line dividing one side of the city from the other. They told me to strip off, and after searching my clothes for money, made me go upstairs, into the street, naked. I felt ashamed. Then they told me to run across the street. I was afraid, there was machine-gun fire. It was one of the most dangerous places in town. They said: "If you don't run we're going to shoot you." I realized that if I stayed I would certainly die, and if I ran maybe I would die. So I ran. Naked, amongst bullets. The soldiers from the side I was running towards stopped shooting and someone came out to meet me. I don't remember the face. He gave me a soldier's uniform to wear. I couldn't speak, couldn't feel my legs. He had to dress me, like a child.

'When I crossed into the other side of town I saw that the people were hungry and destroyed. I had nowhere to go, and stayed with some friends from before the war, the parents of my former pupils. My wife was in Croatia at that point and I had no way of contacting her. She thought I was dead. She had heard from our neighbours that soldiers had taken me away with guns, that they marched me through the neighbourhood for everyone to see. So I decided that I had to get out of there, that I would go mad if I stayed. The only way to get out of the city was over the hill that stood on the east side, but it was heavily guarded. Some people told me that others had managed to escape over that hill, but that you had to crawl during the night, because that was the only way you would avoid being seen. A large spot of a searchlight inspected the hill side. Those who were caught were shot.

'I left at dusk, with a small flask of water strapped on to my belt and bread stuffed into my socks. The road to the foot of the hill was full of sniper alleys and I had to sneak through deserted buildings and ruins, where there were dozens of stinking dead bodies. I thought that they might have been trying to crawl to the other side too. When it got dark enough I started to crawl, and hid in the bushes when the searchlight landed close to me. I crawled for eight hours. It was cold. My trousers were ripped, my skin bled. In the morning I rang up a friend who drives an ambulance. He agreed to pick me up and drive me across the border. I pretended to be a comatose patient and nearly had a heart attack when they opened the door to check what was inside. But they let us go. I slept in the ambulance and awoke thinking I was dead.

'We crossed into Croatia and around noon we arrived in the house where my wife was. She fainted when she saw me, she thought I was resurrected, with wounds and bandages. I had to keep a low profile, in case anyone reported me. I was not welcome in Croatia either, but at least I was safe. I had enough money saved to come here, to the United Kingdom, to seek asylum, with my wife.'

A testimony

One immigration officer pushed the STOP button on the tape recorder. The other two pressed their pens to their lips and regarded Mr H silently. The officer with the tape player stood up and said: 'Thank you Mr H, I will bring Ms Alawi in and she will take you to fill out some more forms.' I translated. Mr H nodded. The stuffy room was momentarily invaded by a wave of office noise from the outside, as the door opened and closed. The men with the pens doodled on their pads and Mr H breathed noisily.

Mr H and I were from the same town. As a child, I'd played at the spot which was now the front line and where he had been stripped naked and told to run. There was a white stone fountain there, shaped like a flower with petals missing on one side; you could also see it as a hand with some of its fingers chopped off. It was built to commemorate the combattants who'd lost their lives in the Second World War. My school friends and I used to run around the fountain, splashing one another with its water in the hot summer afternoons. Afterwards, we'd go home and eat sweet watermelon or juicy cucumber salad. All my memories of that place were soaked in the bleaching Herzegovinian sunshine. Near the fountain was a street where the youngsters hung out in front of bars and cafés, trying to spot whoever it was they had a crush on. Now the soldiers took civilians there, humiliated them, robbed them, and then told them to run or else they'd shoot – and then shot anyway. In my head, nothing fitted together and I wondered if perhaps in fifteen years' time children would play there once again, and Mostar would forget its past and start anew. Or perhaps not.

The door opened and a woman came in. 'Mr H?' The man stood up. 'I am Ms Alawi and I will take you to fill in some papers.' I translated. 'Come with me,' she said. We followed her down the long narrow corridor.

Blinded

One weekend, Milena came over from Birmingham to stay with us for a couple of days. She and Nada had been friends back in Bosnia. They had met on holiday in Croatia some ten years before, and maintained a friendship through occasional visits between Banja Luka, where Milena was from, and Mostar. Milena was a lively woman with wiry red hair and a thunderous cackle that sent the glasses atremble inside the cupboard. She had come to the UK a few months before us, also on a convoy organized by a local volunteer group. As we sat around our kitchen table on Saturday morning having many cups of coffee and dozens of cigarettes, she took out a double newspaper sheet from her diary and said: 'Read this,' to Nada and me. There were two articles, the date was last month's, and the name of the newspaper was unfamiliar to me – some local Birmingham gazette. I read:

Bluebird

Eric Ericsson, solicitor, found dead in his car after a heavy accident. It is suspected that Mr Ericsson lost control of his vehicle after turning a corner on a countryside road at high speed. His body was found by a farmer, Mr P.G. and medical reports indicate that he died of serious head injuries. Mr Ericsson leaves behind his loving wife Penelope and daughters Rachel and Fiona.

And on the opposite page:

A happy reunion of a Bosnian family: wife saves husband from 'living hell'.

Below the headline was a picture of a Yelena Yelenovich, smiling beside an exhausted and elderly looking man. Yelena recalled the story of her terrifying journey, and said that with love and devotion anything is possible.

There was another picture, of a concentration camp near Banja Luka; emaciated men looked out over a barbed-wire fence. Nada and I read and said: 'Yes, we've seen this before. It's too dreadful.'

Milena nodded, adding: 'Yes, but pay attention to this – Eric Ericsson was the man who brought us over to the UK. Yelena Yelenovich is a good friend of mine. They were lovers until that day, when she rescued her husband

and Ericsson drove off the road. Isn't it strange that their stories are on opposite pages?'

We weren't sure, but Milena carried on anyway. 'They started their affair almost straight after their arrival in the UK. People gossiped about it, though no one was sure what was going on – apart from me. Yelena was with Eric just for the sex, it was never about love for her. And then, Yelena's husband was taken to a camp, and Eric helped her go to Bosnia to rescue him without her asylum claim being affected. There were a lot of bitter people in the Bosnian community when that happened,' she said. 'Lots of people wanted to go back and help their families, but everyone was too afraid of breaking their claim.' She paused. 'The worst thing was that I helped Ericsson at work – I was a legal secretary back in Bosnia and I asked him to give me a few hours a week so that I could learn the terminology here, so that when I could start working, I would have something on my CV. That's how I saw everything – and what I didn't see I heard from either him or her.

'I remember him sitting in his cramped square office a few days before he died. The window faced a cobbled street and Eric Ericsson just sat and stared out of the window for hours. He was a tall, skinny man, around fifty. His life changed a lot after he helped bring us to the UK. He must have been sitting there, in his office, cursing the night he decided to organize the convoy. He told me, one time, that he'd watched the news and saw people fleeing their homes, children crying, flames from the burning houses rising into the night like his wife's hair in the wind. He'd walked out into the icy air of his back garden that night and taken deep breaths until small icicles formed on his beard. But nothing could put out the fire of his determination. That's how he put it. I admired him for his sense of urgency. He changed our lives, after all. Well, and his own.

'He liked to recall the morning after he'd made his decision. Sometimes when I went into his office to deliver some papers he wanted, he'd offer me a cup of tea and I'd sit down and listen to him explaining how he'd entered the building where he worked and bolted up the stairs to his office, how he'd contacted several aid agencies, called his local government representatives, arranged some interviews and printed out sheets of paper that read:

WANTED: HELP THE BOSNIANS
ORGANIZATION LOOKING FOR VOLUNTEERS.
PLEASE CONTACT ERIC ERICSSON FOR
INFORMATION. PEOPLE FROM ALL WALKS
OF LIFE WELCOME

and stuck them around town on lampposts and notice boards in shops like Safeway and Oxfam. The next day, one of his assistants stuck her head through the office door and announced that there were a couple of people downstairs who wanted to speak to him about the Help the Bosnians Organization. He said that the assistant had pronounced "Help the Bosnians Organization" with a slight wince implying she thought it was some kind of a mistake. Then there were meetings, followed by the collecting of funds, and then Eric and eight others boarded two rented coaches and drove to the former Yugoslavia. There would only be women and children on board; no men were allowed out of the country.

'He said he noticed her immediately. I'm not surprised. Yelena is an attractive woman, in her mid-forties, small, elfin, with pert breasts. She has this wide smile that men just love. Back in Banja Luka, there were lots of men who wanted to be her lovers, but Yelena didn't care, though she did enjoy the flirting. She loved her husband. But it was different here. Eric was good for her – he helped her forget what was happening and gave her back some of her confidence. She had to look after three kids on her own – boys, aged eleven to fifteen – so she welcomed a fling. But for him, she was the only thing he could think about. His marriage was long dead, though he and his wife were still living together, and he said he was fascinated by how strong Yelena was, how cheerful despite all the things she'd been through. Only she wasn't so cheerful, in fact. Yelena didn't really talk about her problems with Ericsson; Ericsson was the part of her life when she wasn't living her life for a few hours. Her husband had stayed behind in Banja Luka, he couldn't get out. He was a Muslim and Yelena was worried about what would happen to him. But there wasn't much she could do from here. Yelena called her husband once a week, on a mobile telephone owned by some criminals who made money by charging crazy sums for incoming calls. The line was bad, it echoed and crackled and they had to repeat most of what they said twice. It was costly for both of them, but they had to keep in touch somehow. Normal phone lines had been down for months.

'Anyway, Ericsson told me that he fell in love with Yelena immediately. He said that when the bus was parked in a petrol station and he was stranded in his seat, he wished to run up the stairs, take Yelena Yelenovich in his arms and carry her away from everything. "You *were* taking her away from everything," I told him. But I guess he wanted to take her away so they could be alone, just the two of them. He was like a teenager, so in love, as if he'd never been hurt. Otherwise he was such a sensible man. After the journey, Yelena came to the office almost every day. She knew she was safe to come in because I was there and no one would know. He introduced her to Earl Grey tea, which Yelena developed a taste for immediately. She would come up to his office, slip into the small space with a gentle knock on the door and they would drink coffee and tea and eat whatever sweets she brought that day. She is excellent at making sweets, you should try them – cinnamon swirls, chocolate truffles, almond niblets, anything you wish, she can make it. They spoke about books and life and their families. He told her about his daughters and how empty his life had become when they moved away, how saddened he was that one of them, Rachel, had married a Hell's Angel and that Fiona, his younger daughter, turned into a man-hating lesbian. He'd lost all contact with them, and saw them only for Christmas when they all gathered to spend a painful two days together. "It always takes me until Easter to recover from the trauma," he said and they laughed. "My wife and I have grown apart," he added, "we never talk any more. Not like this." Yelena smiled, embarrassed, and he said no more.

'One day he invited her to the woods nearby, where artists sculpted pieces that blended with nature. He wanted her to see the artwork hidden in the trees. Her kids were at school and he'd promised they'd get back before they finished their classes. He brought her a collection of poems by T. S. Eliot that he'd picked up in a nearby bookshop. They drove to the woods slowly. As soon as he parked the car at the entrance to the forest, he took her hand in his and said: "Close your eyes, I have a present for you." She obeyed and he pressed T. S. Eliot into her hand, the small volume slippery from the sweat of his nervous palm. She felt the book, eyes still closed, and Ericsson plunged forth and kissed her. They made love in the forest, in a secret spot he knew, among maple trees. She left the book of poetry in my house that day, so that no one would see it and ask questions.

'Almost eight months after their affair had started, Eric Ericsson sat in his office and watched the street below. It had rained all day and water was running down the kerb, glistening and falling into the drain. Yelena had come to his office the day before and announced that her husband had been taken to a concentration camp. She asked Ericsson to help her return to Bosnia to rescue her husband, and bring him back to England. She said her husband could perish like a beast at any point, and she was the only person who could get him out. All he had to do, she said, was contact the Home Office and arrange for them to let her leave and come back without disturbing her asylum claim, and make sure her husband could join her claim.

'"But what about us?" he asked her. She regarded him silently. It looked as if she had ceased to breathe. And then she said: "But we can still meet and be together, don't worry." His life seemed shattered. "Let me see what I can do. Come and see me in a couple of days," he said and then got up, knelt before her, and they made love on the small client sofa.

'He later told me that as soon as he had asked Yelena Yelenovich that question, it was clear to him that she didn't love him. But he thought that maybe if he helped her, she'd change her mind. I told him: "Eric, the only man Yelena Yelenovich loves is her husband." I wanted to be straight with him – I saw no point in harbouring false hope. "But why is she with me then? We're happy when we're together," he said. "That has to stand for something." "We're all made of many layers, Ericsson," I told him. "Every person is like an artichoke." He just looked out of the window as if something from the outside world might interfere and erase the fact that he could never have Yelena Yelenovich the way he wanted to.

'I remember him dialling the Home Office number. I admired him for doing it – he knew that by helping bring over Yelena's husband, he would effectively be depriving himself of the woman he loved. He spoke to an old friend of his who worked at the Home Office and whom Yelena had once had dinner with, when she and Ericsson had gone to London for a weekend. Her kids were on a school trip and she used the chance to get away.

'He explained the situation quietly and finally added: "Can you see that the woman goes there and brings her husband back to the UK without disturbing her claim?" I saw that he was exhausted by the words. He put the phone down and picked it up again, dialling Yelena Yelenovich's number. "It's me. The man from the Home Office says it's possible." She said she was coming over. Ericsson sat and waited for her in his chair, unable to move, wishing for her to hurry up and wanting never to see her again.

'After Yelena Yelenovich left for Bosnia, the two of them had no contact. Weeks were as slow as 500-year-old tortoises and Ericsson almost never left his office for fear of missing her phone call. He asked me every day: "Have you heard from Yelena?" and I'd say "No, and I don't expect to, for a while." But she did call me once, and said that Bosnia was chaos, like nothing she'd ever seen before. She said she was trying to get her husband out, bribing everyone she knew, but it was hard. She sounded terrible and I wasn't sure if she'd survive the whole thing psychologically. I never told Ericsson that she had called.

'Yelena phoned me again when she came back to the UK. I was in the office. She had managed to get her husband out; he was in a terrible state. Just before we finished the call, I told her she had to speak to Ericsson. "He hasn't left the office in weeks – he just goes home to sleep at night. He's waiting for you to call, Yelena." "I can't do this right now," she said, but then she changed her mind and said: "Put me through to him." I told Ericsson that Yelena was on the line. I imagined him trembling at his desk when he heard her voice.

'"Eric?" she said. "Hello."

'"Yelena. Your voice is so sober and sharp. I've missed you so much."

'I kept the phone receiver to my ear and listened to their conversation. I couldn't resist.

'Yelena said: "We are here. It was hell, but he is alive. I will see you soon. Thank you."

'"I will see you soon?! What does that mean? When?!" His voice surprised him. He added, hurriedly: "I'm sorry, I didn't mean to shout when you called. It's just that I've been waiting to hear from you for so long."

'She said nothing.

'"When are you coming back?" he asked.

'"We are staying in London for the night and catching the early train. I have to go now. Goodbye."

'"Yelena Ye . . ." But she had hung up the phone.

'Several hours later, Ericsson came out of his office and told me he wanted to confront her. "That's a terrible idea," I said. "Wait until things settle down a bit, and then talk to her. She's been through a lot." But he went anyway, and sat in his car, outside her house, waiting for her from 7 a.m. the next day. She didn't turn up until noon. I wonder if Ericsson was surprised at the husband's physique when he finally saw them – we're always jealous of someone we think is better looking than us, superior in some way – Yelena's husband was a walking carcass. She told me what happened afterwards: Ericsson sat in his car, watching them. He'd parked close to their front door and she tried to walk past him as if she had never seen him or the car before. "I didn't expect to see him there," she said, "he frightened me. I know we'd had an affair and I wasn't without feelings for him, but going back to Bosnia ripped my heart out. I felt so guilty, ashamed."

'Yelena Yelenovich opened the door, and her husband disappeared in their children's embraces; she said she had to get something from a shop and came back outside. She approached Ericsson's car and asked, in a quiet voice. "What are you doing here?" He was breathing quickly and grabbed her hand, his fingers like claws. "I wanted to see you," he said. "I haven't slept all night. I've been waiting since seven this morning."

'"Since seven? What for?"

'"I love you. I want to be with you. I wanted to remind you of who I am, that I exist."

'At that moment, Yelena said, Ericsson was pathetic, pitiful, hateful; his yearning repulsed her.

'"Eric, I have just been to hell and back. Can't you understand that? Why are you behaving like a teenager? Now is not the time for all this drama. My husband is here and he has suffered a lot."

Blinded

'"Come with me, come right now," said Ericsson. "We could head out to the woods, where we first made love."

'"You're crazy," she said. And that was it: she walked into the house and closed the door. He drove off, blinded by a denied love.'

The lorry driver

It was August 1993, nine months since we'd arrived in the UK. Our stay seemed increasingly open-ended and my mother was worried that I was too young to be living on my own – I was still only sixteen – and she didn't think it was right that I should stay with another family for longer than a few months. My father never even considered the idea of leaving Mostar, a city he was umbilically tied to, but that summer my mother decided to come to Britain to join me. She was working on the same assumption as the rest of us – that things would settle down soon and we'd all go back home together. When she told me the news, I was desperate to meet her at the airport. The thought of seeing my mother again was life-affirming, as if her mere presence would deliver me into existence once again. As the time since my arrival in Penrith grew and my life became increasingly different from what it had been in Bosnia, combined with my not speaking Serbo-Croat that much and the absence of any old friends, I started to doubt the reality of my memories, and my identity. I sometimes lay in bed in my makeshift bedroom at the vicarage, imagining my Mostar apartment, going over the titles on the bookshelves, the pictures on the walls, the smell of my bed and the sounds I remembered from the outside. I tried to recall a different detail each time, so that my present life wouldn't blot everything out.

I didn't have enough money for the bus or the train to meet my mother at Heathrow, so my friend Johnny arranged for his lorry-driver friend to give me a lift on his way down south. I thought this was a great idea, but I was somewhat dismayed when he told me he'd drop me off on the side of the road somewhere where it was 'really easy to find the way to the Metro' – he used the French word because he was worried I wouldn't know what 'underground' meant.

I met Johnny on the trip from Split – he drove one of the coaches of our convoy, but he was really a lorry driver. He was a short, stocky man with a friendly smile flashing beneath his handlebar moustache. When he first saw me getting on that bus in Split, he grinned and shot a wink in my direction. I seemed a sweet kid, he'd later say. I actually looked as if I had just been released from Auschwitz. I had cropped my hair with amateurish randomness, in 'protest at the war', as I used to put it, and thanks to the food we ate at the public kitchens in Croatia, I was gaunt and half-starved. The kitchens, run by fellow refugees and sponsored by Caritas, featured a weekly menu that consisted of three dishes rotating through the week: macaroni cheese, mouldy salami and bread, tinned tomato soup and bread. We looked forward to the macaroni cheese, which we used to accompany with a glass of water before and after the meal, to fill us up.

There were occasions when, completely broke and still hungry after our meals, my best friend and I would go shoplifting for chicken pâté, having stuffed our pockets with bread slices (there was always plenty of bread). It was easy to steal packs of pâté because they were small, flat and light in the pockets, and we'd complement our lunch with slices of dark bread with thinly spread pâté on top. Occasionally there'd be the delight of see-through slices of cucumber to take off the dryness. We'd eat and watch the sea and the sunset from our little balcony.

Johnny and I became friends because I used to go to his house in Penrith and listen to his stories, sometimes alone, sometimes with Nada and Sasha. He would let Sasha play with the video camera. We'd sit on the floor by his coffee table, he in a white tank top revealing a hairy front and back, talking and drinking cans of beer. On the mound of his six-month-pregnant beer belly, beneath the white cotton, the dark circle of his belly-button hole was visible and looked like a plug.

I was excited about the journey, and on the morning of my trip to London I was enthusiastic about everything, including the struggle to step up inside the lorry. It was the highest I'd ever sat in the front of a vehicle, barring the double-decker on which we'd arrived in England. Unlike that journey, this trip felt more personal, I felt more in control (at least I knew where London was) and the occasion was joyous. The lorry seemed like the man's home, with pictures of his family stuck on the walls and the possibility of making cups of tea using the tiny kettle on the floor.

Johnny's friend Neil, the lorry driver, was short and bald, with endless patience for my bad English. He played Scottish folk songs on the small tape recorder that stood balanced on the dashboard with the aid of heavy-duty brown tape. We took breaks at roadside lorry stops on the way down, and most of them looked the same: the walls and chairs were HP sauce brown and the tables salad cream white. The drivers walked in with smiles, greeting their lonesome road-bound colleagues with slaps on the bare shoulders or handshakes that hurt. They ravished the greasy food and I listened to them talk and understood nothing. I guessed they must have been happy to exchange information about road conditions and whatever they had heard on the radio. I liked the sense of unity they shared and imagined the loneliness they must feel when they parted.

My task on the trip was to turn the cassette over when it had finished, and I had some trouble completing this since the PLAY button was missing and all that was left was a small metal tooth that dug into my skin. The sound coming from the player was tinny, but Neil didn't mind. He knew every song and sang in high-pitched warbles and low-toned coos. He told me that the reason he was so short was because he was ill when he was a child and 'it stunted his growth'.

'What does it mean "stunted"?' I asked.

'Oh, when you're not able to grow nemoore.' (I didn't know what that meant either, but I was too focused on 'stunted' for the moment.)

'You see,' he carried on, 'my mother is 6'5, my father 6'7, my sister's 6'1 and my brothers 6'7 each. My wife is 6'3 and my boy, oh, he's almost 6'4.' The Scottish bag-pipes wailed under his speech.

'What's 6'5 in centimetres?' I asked.

'Oooh, that's a hard one, love. I don't know. Three metres?'

I imagined giants.

'That is not humanly possible. It is too tall.' I said in my best English.

'No, they are so tall, believe me, love.' He looked wist-fully at the road unwinding before him, wishing he was taller. 'Go on darlin', make some tea, the kettle's down there,' he said, as if the tea would alleviate all his sorrows.

I reached for the small dirty kettle on the floor, careful not to scald myself with the boiling water. I thought about my mother and whether she would have aged visibly and what funny thing I might say when I met her, so as not to cry. The road was wide through the large window, the sky grey with patches of blue.

When we reached the vicinity of Heathrow airport, Neil stopped on the side of the road and we said our goodbyes. 'I love your lorry,' I remember saying, my joy at my mother's arrival flooding everything with glittery exuberance. He said a sincere 'Take care of yourself, love,' a greeting that always lingered with me after someone uttered it. My mother and I were to stay with some family friends in London, and I never saw Neil again.

The lorry wobbled off in its immensity down the road, and I walked into Heathrow. When I saw my mother approaching I was surprised she didn't look a hundred years older than when I'd last seen her. I'd had this idea of turning up with a false pregnant belly, a joke on the nine months that had passed between us, a prank that was meant to convey that an entire new life could have – and had, though not physically – come into being since we parted. I'd ditched the joke as soon as I thought of it, but I told her about it when we stopped hugging, salty tears rushing down my cheeks.

Bosnian *Kama Sutra*

My mother's best friend, who'd travelled on another convoy, a year later than me, lived in Exeter, and nine months after arriving in Britain, I moved to Devon. We'd agreed that because I was young I would find it easy to settle down and make friends in a new city and so I moved to Devon, as far south as it was possible to be from Penrith. We stayed with my mother's friend for four weeks, until we found our own flat in a small street with towering ash trees. I suffered for the first couple of months in Exeter, grieving for yet another set of friends snatched away from me by circumstances. I spent a lot of time watching *Prisoner: Cell Block H* on late-night television. The city felt alien, its streets empty after dark. My mother and I went for walks in the day, and I saw the locals glance at us suspiciously when they heard us speaking our language. Whereas I'd felt integrated and comfortable in Penrith, I was once again a foreigner here, ablaze with differentness.

With time, I made friends at school – a group of three girls and three boys – but we had little in common apart from cigarettes. They had large houses in the country-side, two parents, dogs and lots of board games in the cupboards that they took out to play in the wintry nights in front of the fire. I visited some of them a couple of times, but this made me feel alien and I couldn't wait to get back to our flat and the ash trees on our street. One of the boys drove a convertible 4×4 and had a surfing board sticking out of the back; he was all long hair with bleached ends and had a muscular body, and all the girls in our class were in love with him. I sat quietly while my girlfriends worried about make-up, boys and being fat. I didn't wear make-up, didn't like any of the boys around and was way too skinny. Each day, I went home to my mother, who sat worrying about the latest death count on the six o'clock news or held an incomprehensible letter or bill in her hand. I thought I saw her age a year each day.

My friendships at the school slowly petered out, and I ended up socializing mainly with the other Bosnians who lived in Exeter. And this is when I met one of the most spectacular members of the Bosnian diaspora: Bakira, a woman of forty, who came to share a house with a friend of mine for six months.

Bakira had found her way to the UK and Exeter

through John, her husband-to-be, a former UN worker who had picked her up in his big UN lorry one day, when she and her friend were hitchhiking to her home town in eastern Bosnia. John, a shy Englishman who didn't part with words easily, also shared the small Exeter house with my friend and Bakira, his lover and wife-to-be. His present wife, whom he was divorcing, was keeping their marital house in the north of England and John therefore had no home, and was forced to live like a student – or indeed, a refugee.

The day Bakira arrived I was at their house. She was a short, stocky woman, her hair curly and tight around her skull, undoing the locks on the suitcase with her thick worker's fingers. The first things she took out of her luggage defined Bakira immediately. She pulled out and dusted: a framed picture of Tito, which lay on top of her bag; a Bosnian coffee grinder, wrapped carefully in a woollen sweater; and, out of a SPAR plastic bag, a bottle of English cider. She hung Tito's picture on the wall, ground some coffee, poured a glass of cider and, waiting for the water to boil so that she could make the coffee, sat down at the table with us.

'I have a daughter in Zagreb,' she said. 'She lives with my sister. A teenager, she's so clever, she's the best student in her school.' She smoked and her lungs made wheezing noises when she inhaled. 'I want to earn money here to send to her so she can have a bit of fun, you know.

Bosnian *Kama Sutra*

I had her with Rade. He was an army officer in the old Yugoslavia. We met when I was working as a laundress for the army. Oh, he was a sex bomb, my Rade.' John walks in. Bakira changes the subject.

Bakira and John were planning to get married as soon as John's divorce papers came through, and the whole Bosnian-Exeter group became involved in helping arrange the wedding. We spent time at their house on a daily basis, cleaning, sewing, washing, cooking. Bakira always worked with a glass of cider by her side, her skin doughy and sallow from smoke and cheap alcohol.

One of the greatest mysteries of Bakira and John's relationship was the fact that she spoke no English, and he understood very little Bosnian. In the mornings, when she got up and started brewing her dynamite coffee, followed by John in thin white pyjamas scraping the floor with the soles of his slippers, she would say in Bosnian: 'John, it's not going to work like this. The sex is just not good enough – you come quickly and me – nothing! But you don't care, do you? You have to spend more *time*, you hear?' My friend, their housemate, would pretend to be reading the paper, embarrassed.

Bakira's effort to make herself more understandable to John consisted of adding an English intonation on top of Bosnian words. John would be silent, staring at the floor. Did he understand? No one knows.

When I visited my friend, Bakira would invariably

offer coffee and tell us things like: 'Ha, me and Rade, we used to have such good sex. We would take an erotic magazine and we would go through each position. One by one! With John, nothing. Always the same. Him on top, me below, and that's it. He comes and I'm left there like a wet cloth. There's no one like Rade, but he's in Serbia, what can I do? John is a good man, but he's a bit quiet you know? And me – a wet cloth.' And she would lean forward with her coffee, cider and cigarette breath. 'You know?'

'Yes,' I used to say, although my early teenage years had not enlightened me on what it was like to be left there like a wet cloth.

Once, when there had been a particularly bad day in Bosnia and reports on TV spoke of many dead and injured, Bakira said, without peeling her eyes from the screen: 'Thank God I never lost a limb in the war. Who would have fucked me without a leg?' We sat speechless, unbelieving, and John got up and left the room. Perhaps he understood more than we thought.

I got drunk with Bakira once, and I think that was the closest I will ever get to experiencing the atmosphere in a Bosnian *kafana*, a bar for men only where hard liquor is served, and women with bleached hair dance unglamorously on tabletops. It was Bakira's birthday and I went round for a morning coffee. My mother was waiting for me at home to help her send a food parcel to Bosnia, so I couldn't stay for longer than half an hour. But Bakira pleaded: 'Come on, it's my birthday, let's have a glass of vermouth!' I said OK, but only one, it's too early in the morning for this, or something to that effect. We had a glass, and another glass, the sun was just reaching its noon blaze and I was getting drunk. I'd never drunk that early in the day, but it was Bakira's birthday and she was alone and I couldn't say no. She was talking about her daughter and I stuck around and listened to her proud stories. Around lunchtime we bought another bottle of vermouth. Bakira pulled a cassette out of the 'special pocket' of her suitcase and put it on, first winding it on with her fat finger, because it was tangled inside. Folk songs poured from the round speakers, and Bakira climbed on the plastic white kitchen table, lifted her arms to the sky and danced in circles, singing at the top of her voice. I was laughing, and drunk.

When my mother rang the doorbell it was already late afternoon and I was in my friend's bed, my head heavy, unable to move. Just as Bakira had reached a climax with her song, I had run to the toilet and vomited, my friend holding my head. Since then I'd been lying on the bed, in the shoes and coat I hadn't taken off, trying to stop everything from spinning round. Bakira's wailing voice still filled the kitchen: 'I am a Yuuugoooslaaaaav!' My mother's furious ringing of the bell prompted a sudden silence and an attempt at hiding the bottles (unsuccessful).

Bluebird

My friend sat on the sofa pretending to read the newspaper (upside down), and Bakira grabbed some piece of sewing she was working on, the wrong way round at first, the threads hanging limply, her eyelids drooping, her breath poisonous. My mother looked at the empty bottles of vermouth betraying our morning excesses and then found me on the bed.

'Get up,' she said.

'I can't. My head can't.' I gargled.

'It's my birthday today! Have a drink, c'mon!' Bakira said to my mother, unwisely trying to change tactics.

'This is disgusting!' My mother slammed the door as she left.

When Bakira got married everyone danced around to one of her cassettes. John didn't speak much at the wedding. He danced shyly, limply moving his legs to the atrocious folk rhythm. I had no insight into the mind hiding beneath his ashen hair, and wondered what he thought his new wife was saying when she uttered her Bosnian words dipped in an Anglophonic sauce. She did not wear white, and when the party was in full swing she brought out her picture of Tito and danced with it above her head, probably thinking of Rade.

Friendship

In the winter of 1993 life in Croatia was bleak; there were no jobs nor money, and no prospects of either. The lack of everything had been easier to face in the August sunshine, but winter increased the quotidian harshness. My mother had been desperate for my sister, who had left Penrith in 1992 to return to her boyfriend, to come back to the UK and continue her education. Now, in October 1993, exactly a year after we'd docked in Dover with the Lake District group and less than twelve months after she had left the UK, my sister arrived in Exeter. There was a brief legal wrangle with the Home Office, after which she was allowed to seek asylum for the second time, together with her boyfriend.

Their arrival was preceded by one of the strangest friendships – if it could be called that – I've ever experienced. The Bosnian group in Exeter had arrived in a similar way to those of us who had travelled to the Lake District: a local volunteer group had driven to Croatia, picked them up, housed them, and so on. Part of this group was a middle-aged couple, Jack and Myra. Jack and Myra hadn't actually travelled to Croatia, but they volunteered to befriend the Bosnian families and help them practise their English by visiting them in their homes. Jack was a tall man with a bald head, aviator-shaped glasses and thin lips, inseparable from his camera. Myra wore the large spectacles often worn by myopic snooker players, and a weavy, hair-sprayed golden beehive. She was a nurse and had a kind expression. Both were in their early fifties and had been together, they said, for thirty years.

When we arrived in Exeter, Jack and Myra had already been visiting the other Bosnian families for some months. The first time they came to us they were introduced by another Bosnian family, and we all sat in our living room, talking about the war and the latest news. Jack and Myra listened to my translation of the conversation and nodded a lot. They stayed for a couple of hours and, as they were leaving, they said they'd call us and come round again. We nodded approvingly, but after they left, my mother and I agreed we weren't sure what to make of them; however, their visits seemed to be the order of the day in the Bosnian community, and I thought it might be nice to make some local friends. From then on, Jack and Myra would phone every Monday and Wednesday evening to confirm that they were visiting the following day. The phone would ring around 6 p.m. The conversation was always the same:

'Hello Vesna, it's Jack here.'

'Hello Jack, how are you?'

'I'm very well, and how are you?' he'd say slowly.

After I replied I was very well too he'd say: 'Myra and I were thinking of coming over tomorrow evening. Is 7 p.m. fine for you?'

Feeling a heaviness in my stomach, I'd agree: 'Yes, of course. See you tomorrow.' I never said no, even if I'd planned to earlier in the day.

My mother and I had soon tired of their visits but the truth was that we were almost always home, and they knew it. We had little money and the deserted night streets of Exeter were eerie, so we had cut out our habit of evening walks. My mother would read in the living room or write letters, while I did my homework, played the guitar badly, and read books. Often we sat together on the sofa and talked, mostly reminiscing about times gone by since nothing was going on in our daily lives. Sometimes the other Bosnians came to visit us, and we'd put some money together for a bottle of wine and have dinner. Apart from that, Jack and Myra's Tuesday and Thursday visits constituted our only concrete evening plans.

Because my mother didn't speak enough English to be

able to hold her own conversations, I had to translate. But Jack and Myra didn't talk much, and my mother didn't know what to talk to them about, so I found myself inventing subjects for conversation. I tried talking about anything. The TV was invariably on, and I commented on the colour of someone's hair, what they were wearing, or a product that was being advertised. I was indefatigable in my attempts to liven up our time together and break down the stout and indelible boredom. I tried starting philosophical discussions – something that everyone might contribute to – asking questions like: 'Do you think God exists?' or 'Are you a cat or dog person?' But nothing worked. Sometimes I took out my guitar and played 'Starry, Starry Night' by Don McLean, a song about the genius of Van Gogh and what a shame it was that he took his own life. I sang too, and my mother always claimed to enjoy it, though my repertoire was extremely limited (there were, in all, about four songs I could play). Jack and Myra smiled while I sang, applauded, and sat back with their lips zipped up.

One day, my mother decided to employ her own tactic to enliven our time with Jack and Myra and made dinner; she figured we could kill an hour by eating together. This only made matters worse, though, because Jack and Myra then attempted to increase their visits to three times a week. Desperate at the prospect, we wangled out of the third by inventing chores, but the two stock drop-ins remained. They'd come round, we'd exchange greetings and howareyous, and they'd sit down on the sofa, the weight of their silence dropping in the room like a bloated carcass. My mother would serve dinner in the kitchen and we'd sit around the table, eating, the clinks of glasses, forks and knives audible against the convulsing ash trees in the wind outside, or the tinkle of rain on the tin window sill. After dinner, we would move to the living room and Jack and Myra would sink into the sofa and watch TV. My mother got some relief by washing the dishes and listening to the music on the radio for fifteen minutes or so, while I sat with Jack and Myra, talking about the latest Head & Shoulders advert, asking questions like: 'Is it possible that anyone has so much dandruff?' Anything was better than the silence.

About an hour after dinner, Jack would produce his camera and ask us to smile. My mother and I would expose our teeth and gaze at the lens, and Jack would click twice, the strong flash blinding us temporarily. This, we later learned, he did with all the Bosnian families. The photos were terrible; the flash was too strong, the light in the room was awful, my mother was wrinkled with worry, her hair limp, clothes mismatched and shabby. I was puffy-faced, a teenager with features yet to evolve, always a cigarette between my fingers. Then, on their next visit, after the food and the hour of

TV, Jack would take the photos out of his bag and we'd look at them and pretend we liked them. After they went home, we buried the photos in a dark corner of our drawers.

A couple of months later, all the Bosnians started complaining about the vapidity of Jack and Myra's visits. Most of the adults had enrolled on an English language course, including my mother, though seemingly what they most enjoyed was the time between lessons – the coffee and cigarette breaks when everyone chatted and gossiped. The subject of Jack and Myra came up on one of those breaks. It turned out that, with the exception of Sunday, the couple were visiting Bosnian families every night of the week.

One day I went to pick up my mother from the school so that we could do our weekly shop, and I found all the Bosnians standing outside, puffing away and drinking coffee from plastic cups. Though their ages ranged between forty and seventy, they looked like teenagers on their school break, whispering to each other and gesticulating wildly. They were again discussing Jack and Myra.

'Do you think they are saving on gas and electricity bills by never spending any time at home?' an elderly woman wondered innocently.

'Maybe,' someone said.

'Why would they never want to be in their own home, where they are most comfortable?' asked someone else.

Friendship

'They're certainly not spending any money on food,' Bakira concluded, though she was exempt from their visits because her partner was a native English speaker.

'Who knows, do they actually have a home?' one man asked. 'Has anyone ever been round to their house?' Everyone shook their heads. 'Does anyone know where they live?'

'Somewhere outside town, I think,' said a woman.

'Of course they have a home,' another person said. 'They are always tidy and well dressed.'

There was murmuring among them, and then my mother announced: 'I don't want to have to have them round every week. We have hardly enough money to feed ourselves, yet I've now got them used to dinner twice a week. In the beginning it was helpful, there was always food left over from us and I didn't have to waste it – I've never cooked for two before, what with us being a family of four – but I just can't afford to keep it up.'

Everyone agreed, but no one could think of a polite way to refuse them. I'd never thought about the financial aspect of it – to me they were just boring.

We knew little about Jack and Myra. They had a daughter and a son, both grown up and living elsewhere. Their house was on the outskirts of Exeter, but we didn't know exactly where. One of the only times they revealed personal information was when they announced that Myra was pregnant. She was having twins. We congratulated them in English, though my mother said, in Serbo-Croat, that at fifty-one Myra was too old to have a baby, let alone twins. I didn't translate her comment for the fear of offending them. I wondered secretly when they'd found the time for sex, considering they were never alone and at home, but then I remembered that they kept their Sunday nights free. A few weeks later, Myra said she'd had a miscarriage, but neither of them looked any different from their normal selves. They still made it to our home twice a week, ate dinner, sat on the sofa, watched TV, took photos, brought the photos, smiled at my wailing and guitar playing, and watched the world from behind their glasses.

And so it remained until October, the day before my sister arrived with her boyfriend, when Jack and Myra's visit coincided with that of a couple from Mostar who lived close by. My mother had prepared food, and we sat around our small kitchen table, eating, some conversation going on between my mother and the friends, while I translated things like: 'Oh, they are talking about the price of potatoes,' or 'They say that it's very cold today,' or 'Do you want some more chicken?' to Jack and Myra. Finally, after a few glasses of wine, my mother wanted to say something to them, but knowing that I was prone to censor anything I thought might be too direct, she asked the woman of the Mostar couple to translate – the woman spoke reasonable English and had no vested interest or censorship authority over my mother.

'Since we are all such good friends,' my mother began, 'and since you have visited us so many times, we are interested in visiting your house and seeing where you live.' She paused, then added: 'We want to learn a little about you.' The woman translated and I wondered if my mother was truly interested in the inner depths of Jack and Myra's lives or if she was simply bluffing. 'In Bosnia,' she said, 'this is how friendships work.' Myra listened and stared at the lamb chops glistening on her plate, while Jack nodded. When the translation was finished, he said: 'Myra and I would be delighted to have you round, but we are very busy, so I'll have to check my diary to see when we could receive you.' My mother smiled and we all carried on eating, and the silence, which was always there, was sulkier on Jack and Myra's side; conversation flowed between my mother and the Mostar couple. I decided not to interfere in the silence or the conversation and ate my lamb chops.

When the guests left, I cleared up. There were crimson ringlets on the table cloth where wine glasses had been. Jack and Myra's forks and knives were stacked neatly on top of their plates.

Later we heard that they still visited some of the families regularly, but others took the same route as my mother, asked if they could pay Jack and Myra a visit in their home, and as a result were struck off the visiting list. Jack and Myra never telephoned us, or came to see us again.

January 1994

One frosty morning in Exeter, I woke up to a letter lying on the floor by the front door. Everyone was still asleep, so I sat at our kitchen table by the window and ripped open the envelope. It was dated end of January 1994, in my father's handwriting. Outside, a man walked quickly in the cold, his ears red like corals. I saw my own breath before me, steamy and soft.

My dearest,

It's morning and those bastards on the hills are quiet, so I am writing to you while I can still think. I came out of the hospital two days ago. Thank God, I couldn't stand that food any longer. Our aid packages are much tastier. The neighbour came by and brought some grub from her village, some potatoes like the ones your grandma bakes. The taste brought back so many memories.

Bluebird

So, what's new, you ask. Well, everything is pretty much the same, only we had a small incident in the neighbourhood yesterday. I went to see Muhamed and we had a bit to drink, so we started singing *sevdalinke*. I suppose we were a bit loud and the windows were open, but those stupid boys who guard the buildings, who are now big Croats all of a sudden, came up into the flat and told us to stop singing Muslim songs. I told them to go to hell, that I was a Serb and I was singing it, but that wasn't such a good idea – they nearly arrested me. I had to plead disability so they would leave me alone. So after I left, Muhamed fell asleep and when he woke up his TV was gone. Those little bastards came back and robbed him. That's all they do. They just steal. It's no secret, but what can you do about it? Nothing. Just keep quiet. If you don't, you will end up like that man who was shot by one of those guards recently. You know how they shoot in the air if someone's window is not completely blacked out, as a warning? Well, they were doing that, and this man apparently came out on his balcony and shouted: 'Do you have to shoot all the time? Is this racket ever going to stop?!' And the guard just shot him. 'There you go,' he said, 'now you'll have silence for ever.'

So I try not to go out too much. You have to go and get water, but my leg's not good yet, so someone always brings a bit for me too. A friend came to see me the other day in the hospital and he said that I should watch out, that the soldiers are taking all the remaining Serbs out of their houses and making them dig trenches and sometimes taking them on a leash and making them eat grass. Just to humiliate them. What are people made of, I keep asking myself? Where is all this cruelty and sadism coming from?

That Laura from our neighbourhood still walks around thinking she's a man. Apparently she went to report into the army, to fight and they said: 'No women here Laura.' She was angry after that. She comes to drink with us sometimes. See, at least some people never change. It's only the crazy ones who stay the same around here it seems. And, what's worse, even more crazy ones are springing up every day.

Enough from me and my war chronicles. I'll write again.

Keep well and be cheerful.

And then, soon after that letter was written, my father died. Suddenly and quickly. Seemingly from an earache. We received a phone call one cloudy afternoon telling us that he'd complained of earache a couple of days before and, having been prescribed some pills, he'd taken too many (my father had a strange way of reasoning that if one pill was helpful, ten were even more so), fell into a coma and died in the morning, in the crumbling city hospital. We sat around, silent, not knowing what to do. It was February 1994, and I had been in England for around fourteen months, the time it took a child to learn to walk. My mother, sister and I tried to work out what to do. The first thing we agreed it would be wise to do was arrange a funeral. But who was going to bury him? We were all in Britain and his brothers and sisters were all in Serbia. So, I called the Home Office.

'Hello. Is this the Home Office?'

'Yes. What's your IND Number?'

'30567344.'

'How can I help?'

'I am an asylum seeker, and my father has just died in Bosnia and there is no one there to bury him. I am wondering if there is any possibility of my mother, who is also in Britain and also an asylum seeker, going there to arrange the burial without affecting her claim.'

'Wait a minute, Miss. I'll put you through to the right department.'

Silence. An abrupt ring and then: 'Yes, hello!'

'Hello, my IND Number is 30567344. My father has just died in Bosnia and there is no one there to bury him. I am wondering if there is any possibility of my mother, who is also in Britain and also an asylum seeker, going there to arrange the burial without affecting her claim.'

'I see. And there is no one who might be able to bury him there?'

'No. We are all here and his brothers and sisters are all in Belgrade. My father is Serb and the Orthodox grave-yard is not in use. It is in a very dangerous spot, on a hillside. Nobody else would want to do it. We would have to arrange a burial at a temporary graveyard, outside the city where they bury Muslims and Serbs who die on the west side of the city.'

'I see. And where is this place where he can be buried?'

'I don't know exactly. It's called Medjine. It's next to a village, around ten kilometres outside the city.'

'Can you tell me exactly where it is? Do you have a map?'

I go get a map of Yugoslavia. What the hell does she need this information for? I don't dare ask. She asks the questions, I answer. Even if her questions are ridiculous and irrelevant.

'It's exactly on a green patch not so far from a place called Mostarsko Blato,' I tell her.

'I see.' She's taking notes.

'So, do you think this will be possible?'

'What did he die of?'

'He had a problem with his ear, and then he had a

brain haemorrhage. He fell into a coma in the evening and died in the morning.'

'I see.' More notes.

'So do you think this will be possible? We can't wait for a long time. There's a war going on there and they can't keep bodies for a long time. Nothing works. There is no way to preserve dead bodies. People are buried more or less immediately.'

'Hmhm. Let me review your request with some of my colleagues and I will let you know. What is your telephone number?'

I give it to her.

We wait. We wait another day. We remember a distant relative of my father's who still lives in a village in western Herzegovina. We call him and my mother's brothers and sisters. They all pull together with our neighbours, and bury my father. They take pictures of the body, which I find accidentally in a bunch of photos seven years later, while I'm sitting on the toilet going through a mound of family photographs. Seeing those pictures is a moment I won't forget, for I regret that all things related to my father's death were so mistimed, and nothing was ever done in the way it should have been. The funeral was small: five people, including the little hunchback friend of the family who had been living with my father for a few months and was the one who called an ambulance when he found him unconscious on the bed.

The funeral done, I call Ms Ray, the immigration officer whom I had spoken to some days before.

'Hi, may I speak to Ms Ray please?'

'May I ask who it is and what is it regarding?'

I explain.

'Oh, well, I'm sorry to say but Ms Ray is on holidays for two weeks.'

'And when did she go, if I may ask?'

'About two or three days ago. Is there anything I can help you with?'

'No. Thank you.'

I put the phone down. I visualize myself with a mighty AK47, mowing down all the immigration officers and inflicting a particularly slow and painful death on Ms Ray. This turns into a dream that haunts me for weeks. My father's temporary grave waits for better times on a wide green plain, where cypresses sway in the wind.

Healing is hard. My father's bare bones were moved some years later to the family burial plot at the Orthodox graveyard in Mostar. Every year I visit the grave, which sits on the hillside of barren earth and rocks overlooking the city. Once this graveyard was sheltered by tall pines and cypresses that threw a deep shade on the grey tombstones where black and white photographs of the dead stared into the distance. During the war, the trees were cut down and used as firewood by the freezing people in

Bluebird

the city and someone knocked out bits of the faces in the photographs of the deceased with a chisel, to vent their hatred. Every year I visit and sit on the hot stone of the grave at the end of a sweltering summer day, by the rosemary bush that spills from the gravelly soil. Sometimes I see turtles making slow love in the shrubbery. Sometimes I bring my friends and we gaze at the city below. Sometimes I sit alone and watch other mourning relatives sitting alone at someone else's grave, while the sky changes from light hues to a thick indigo that floods the earth like spilled ink.

A place by the sea

After my father's death, my mother returned to Bosnia and Herzegovina. My sister and I said goodbye to her for the second time in two years, only now it was she who was leaving on a bus, not us. Parting was even harder the second time – just as we'd all got used to being together again, everything was breaking anew. We decided to make the best of it and look forward to our next move – Hull. My sister had got a place at university there and her boyfriend and I followed her up to Yorkshire. I was to move in by myself after the initial few weeks and do my A-levels, while my sister and her boyfriend would live nearby. We'd traced our journey on a map and saw that Hull was near the sea. We dreamed of long beaches and perhaps even palm trees along a promenade. Our naivety knew no end. When a friend's mother asked us 'When are you moving up to hell?' we assumed it was a joke and laughed. The place was by the sea, how bad could it be?

A kind neighbour offered to drive us up in a van. The three of us sat in the back, surrounded by our bags. As we entered Hull our faces revealed the sinking of our hearts. It's fair to say that Hull was where I had my first UK culture shock. The endless rows of terraced houses reminded me of sets for *Monty Python* sketches, the tree-less streets were grim and lifeless, the tireless wind blew apart any semblance of a hairstyle. There was not a hint of Lake District peaks or lushness, no sight like Exeter Cathedral.

We arrived in the house my sister had rented after a brief introductory visit a few months before. It was dark and beer cans lay scattered all over the floor, the remains of the previous tenants' moving-out party. Our Exeter neighbour left us and drove home, and we sat on the sofa and stared at the wall. My sister had got her place at university because another Bosnian girl had dropped out – she had tried to commit suicide. We understood her motivation. I suggested going out for a walk; if we explored the area, perhaps we'd find something nice. We walked around the town centre. It was Sunday and everything was closed except for a pub called Sergeant Pepper's where loud techno was playing and men and women fell out on to the pavement, drunk and vomiting. We went back to the house.

A place by the sea

The next day I walked along the high street watching girls younger than me pushing prams. I was amazed at the supermarket, Kwiksave, where a can of baked beans cost 1p. I went as far as the river that was really the sea, they said, and discovered a lot of mud swaying lethargically under a thin layer of water.

I started studying for A-levels at a local college. My English literature classmates were girls who talked about wanting to work at the Tesco superstore checkouts; my philosophy class consisted of a motley group of several seventy-year-old men determined to grasp the meaning of life and two junkie brothers who used any opportunity to tell the rest of us that drugs were fine. They were nearing forty and trying to complete a philosophy A-level for the tenth time. The art classes were frequently interrupted by a schizophrenic man who became angry when his painting wasn't going well. I befriended an Australian girl who never left the house without a tub of foundation on her face and wearing a very short skirt, so that she got whistled at by builders even at nine in the morning. I, on the other hand, became introverted and quiet and couldn't connect with anything around me. My eighteenth birthday was so uneventful that I can't even remember what I did. I unrequitedly loved the only relatively sane person who came to visit us – a friend we'd made through someone we knew in Exeter – but he wasn't interested in me at all. I wasn't getting on with my sister or her boyfriend, the days were short and dark, and I missed home and my mother. I realized this when I stood in a telephone box while my sister rang my mother and I listened to her crying into the receiver. My sister was always the dramatic one and her feelings took priority because she expressed them with such gusts of temper; I had never stopped to think about what I felt and why. But when I heard my sister saying: 'Mummy, I miss you,' I thought, 'That's it. I miss my mother.'

My mother had left England unhappy and broken by exile. After my father died, soldiers came to expel Mustafa, the small hunchbacked family friend who had been staying with my father. They arrived with machine guns and ordered him to get out, and said that, if he was still there when they came back the next day they would kill him. Scared, he called my uncle, who called my mother, who called my cousin, who was in the special police forces – a decent man, who – everyone said – had never stolen anything or moved into anybody's flat. It was common for people to move into empty flats, even if they already had a place. They would break in and change the locks. It could happen if you left the city or just went out to get some food. There was a case of a man who was so afraid that somebody would move into his flat that he set up a booby trap on his door every day when he went out. One day he met some friends, got drunk, forgot about the booby trap and just opened the door when he got home without defusing the system. He blew himself up like a watermelon.

I'd known Mustafa since I was small. During the Second World War, when he was a child, an army of people had walked over him, breaking his spine and leaving him a hunchback for life. He was a Muslim, in my parents' flat, the home of a Serb and Croat, living on the side of the city controlled by Croats, who would have been more than happy to kill him right there and then, except they knew about my cousin in the special police forces, so they gave him a day to get out. My cousin found the three men who'd gone into our flat and threatened Mustafa, and said something to them, or slapped them about, I like to imagine. They never came back.

After that, my mother returned to Bosnia and got a job. She told us that a bunch of women had come to the house and clucked like chickens around her: 'You don't know how much we suffered, you have no idea, you had it easy in England, it was so hard for us.' She held the front door open and ordered them out. England for her had been filled with worry, poverty, incomprehension and weeping.

Two deaths happened during the year my mother spent in Britain – my father's and a cousin's. The cousin had just got married and his wife was pregnant. He went out with his best friend, who'd been best man at his wedding, and the friend got into an argument with an acquaintance they bumped into in a bar. The dispute was about something trivial, they said, and my cousin stood by. But the arguing became quite heated and suddenly the acquaintance pulled out a gun to make his point more forcefully, fired and missed. The bullet killed my cousin. Everyone carried weapons at that time and resolved arguments by shooting. My mother was devastated, her sister having died the year before, then her nephew, then her ex-husband, and she said she was afraid of everything during the first months back in Mostar.

I knew how she felt because I, too, was also afraid of everything sometimes – of what was and what could be, things that happened or that might happen, and that nothing would change. But then my mother said: 'I have to be strong,' and went swimming every day and got her strength back. I admired her toughness, her survival instinct, her love, and sense of protectiveness. I missed her terribly and lived in perpetual fear that something would happen to her and I wouldn't be able to help her.

I went on a school trip to London with my English class that November and one of the girls announced that she was pregnant. She was sixteen. I asked her: 'So what are you going to do?' and she said she'd keep the baby. I couldn't think of anything worse than having a child so young. I was eighteen and hadn't even had sex yet because I thought I wasn't ready. I asked why she wanted a child now and she said, simply: 'I want someone to love me.' I went to bed that night clutching my Walkman and listening to highly depressing Bosnian music, thinking about my mother. I wondered if being in denial about being depressed was better.

I went to visit friends who lived in South London. They'd invited me to see a video that their son-in-law had made when he was staying with my mother in Mostar. My next-door neighbour, my mother and the young man with the camera had walked around Mostar asking young people questions about what it was like to be living there in 1994. The war was still going on and it seemed as though it would never end. Everything was grey and destroyed. My mother was laughing and they were all cracking jokes. I recognized one of the young men they interviewed. I hadn't really known him well, but in my extreme loneliness I was absorbed by a longing, as if he'd been my best friend. I felt removed from everything – my former life in the former Yugoslavia, my present, empty life in Hull, my possible life anywhere else. I became anxious, afraid of everything, uneasy about daylight and about night-time. I was also feeling very sorry for myself. And I talked to no one about it.

*

Bluebird

In December that year my sister's boyfriend's parents visited us. They didn't stay in our crumbling house with five bedrooms – only two of which were occupied. When we showered the water leaked down into the kitchen via the neon light on the ceiling, creating a light-show. We had a cement garden too, that we looked at out of our living-room window. One evening my sister's boyfriend's parents took us out for dinner at McDonald's. We sat under more neon lights, eating plastic-tasting chips. There wasn't much talking going on, except for occasional mentions of people from their town in Croatia, whom I didn't know. As I sat there, I swore to myself never to eat at McDonald's again, and made a decision right there and then, under the brutally bright lights, on those round faux-leather seats, with the chips in my mouth, that I had to snap out of it. Nothing was going to get better if I carried on pitying myself. I needed to make some friends, quick.

It took a few months, but I came to love Hull. I started listening to the radio – for some reason it made me feel less alone – and I discovered a beautiful park. I came to know the old woman at the launderette who called everyone 'flower' and the shopkeepers who asked about your life when you went in for a pint of milk. I started helping foreign students at my college to improve their English, and I met great people, from Angola, France, Japan, Italy,

Greece, even Mauritius. I made friends with a local hair-dresser and we took Mable, his skinny whippet, for walks on the moors.

I had a Russian friend who drove an uninsured Alfa Romeo with an expired Russian licence. One day he crashed into the parked car of a woman in labour, about to go to hospital, after he'd had a post-lunch drink on his way to his illegal job as a security guard. He thought he'd rot in jail but, luckily for him, the woman didn't press charges. He drove us to the coast once and we walked along the windy beach collecting shells. I liked the mood-iness of the sky and the sea, the crazed gulls that yelled and glided on the wind and the smooth pebbles that clinked in my pocket.

'Get out of my dreams, get into my car'

One of the tallest people I know escaped Bosnia in the boot of a car. I couldn't believe my eyes when I opened the front door and there he was, towering above me, with a big smile, arms grabbing me for a hug and lifting me off the floor. 'Zlatko!' I shouted and my sister came running, incredulous at hearing his name there, in Hull.

He stepped inside the narrow corridor of our house and filled the space entirely. It was as if a moment had not passed since I had last seen him, although it had been two years since my arrival in the UK. Zlatko was a friend from our neighbourhood who lived two buildings from us, on the fifth floor. He used to come and pick me up to go out for a drink, always having to stoop to enter the flat. He had long hair and big ears and a sense of humour like no one else I knew. Whenever he came round to our house, my father said: 'Zlatko, you will live longer than any of us

170

with all that mountain air you're breathing up there.' And Zlatko would laugh and say to my father: 'I can see that your scalp is getting flaky from up here, you may need to get a toupee soon. I'd be happy to help you choose.'

And now here he was, in our house in Hull, thousands of miles away from home.

'How did you get here?' we asked.

'You won't believe it, but I got here in a car boot.'

I tried to picture it: he was 6'7, his legs stretching for ever. It was not physically possible for him to fit into the boot of a car. 'What kind of a car – a lorry?'

'No,' he laughed. 'A BMW. Very comfortable, actually.'

I made coffee and we sat down together. My sister, her boyfriend and I surrounded Zlatko like children around a storyteller, impatient to hear the details of this incredible journey.

'I was mobilized three months ago. I tried hiding first, I didn't want to go and fight, but they found me and enlisted me and sent me to be a watch guard, with my being so tall, they said. Every day, ten, twelve hours, I was sitting in this trench with a view of the entire valley on the west side of the city. I was to alert them if anyone was coming. Some days it was quiet, but others, oh man, it was horrible. Such chaos. People shot, blood, scream-ing, like something from a film. You can't believe it's happening. Some soldiers were getting drunk, stoned and then going for it, charging and shooting like madmen.

'I thought about escaping all the time, it was the only thing I wanted to do. I made some enquiries, and this guy told me about a man on an island in Croatia who transports people across the border for money. I had no idea of the details, but he said the guy had a good success rate and was reliable. But getting out of the city was impossible, I couldn't get a permit to leave the country. Until one day, my lucky soldier star shone on me.

'I was driving back from the stupid trench and I picked up a commander whose car had broken down. He was stranded, and my lift saved him hours of waiting on the empty road. So, because he was so grateful, when he was leaving he said: "Anything I can do for you, mate, just let me know. Here is my card." I wasn't going to let such an opportunity pass. "There is something that would make my life much easier." He listened. "I've got this girl in Croatia, I've been seeing her for some time, and I really want to go and visit her. She doesn't want to come here, she's afraid of the guns and the bombs – you know what girls are like – but she wants to see me. And I need a day's permit to get out of the country, you know, a man's a man, even during a war." I winked at him, all macho and everything. I knew he would love that sort of thing, he was a peasant with thick fingers and a red, drunk's face. He laughed, his lungs wheezing, and said: "I know, mate! No problem. I can do that for you. Come and see me tomorrow afternoon at this address. And we'll have a drink!" He made a drinking gesture, his thumb pointing up and towards his mouth.

'The next day I went to see him. Before that I called this number that I had for the Croatian man on the island. I phoned him from one of those motherfucker expensive mobiles that those bastard profiteers rent. I know one of them, he went to school with me, always was an arsehole. But anyway, I called him and he said: "Yes. OK. Come and see me when you can. I am here all week. I will have the medicine for you." He spoke in "code" you see. I thought it was quite funny, but in a way he was going to give me "the medicine". Getting out was saving my life. All I'd managed to say to him was: "Hi Mr Kokičević – a stupid code name – I am a friend of Stjepan," and he immediately replied in this coded message.

'When I got to the commander's quarters the next day, I was shivering from being so nervous. I was convinced something was going to go wrong, like he won't be able to do it, or he won't remember me, or something. I was sweating and my hands were shaking like fuck. When I came in, he hugged me and slapped me on the back, and gave me a glass of *rakija* to drink. I downed the *rakija* immediately, it was a welcome relief. He poured another glass and said: "Attaboy!" when I downed that one too. "So, who's this lady of yours?" He asked me. "Oh, her name is Maria" – the first name I could think of, like the Virgin – "she's from near Split. A nice girl, I might marry

173

her after the war." I thought of what she might look like, this Maria. "She has long dark hair, beautiful eyes, huge breasts," I volunteered. He was nodding. "So, what are you planning to do when you go over there?" He asked me all these questions, as if to make sure I really did have a girlfriend, which of course I didn't. It was so easy to make her up, this Maria, and I was enjoying creating her so much that by the end of it I wished she really existed. "I had a wife too," he said. "She died before the war. She was Serb," he said. "I wonder what she would have made of this mess. She loved Tito and his politics, always repeated that quote of his 'Cherish Yugoslavia's brotherhood and unity as if they were the apple of your eye.' She'd never have believed this. I was devastated when she died, now I thank God she's not here any more." Then he pulled out a piece of paper. He had the permit ready for me. I thanked him and said sorry about his wife. I didn't have anything else to say. All I wanted was out. I couldn't feel anything for anyone's death any more. And now I think this guy knew I wasn't planning on coming back and he knew there was no Maria, but he took pity on me and decided to help me out.

'I had my bag packed at home, so all I did was pick it up and get into my car. My mother was already in Norway, so I wasn't leaving anyone behind, apart from some friends. But I didn't have time to say goodbye to anyone. I wore my uniform so I would look more official. At the border no one bothered me too much, just some routine questions, but I still had to stop at the nearest bar to go to the toilet, I had had diarrhoea for days now, from nerves. I got to Split in four hours and drove straight to the harbour. When I got there I was told that I'd missed the ferry going to the island that morning, which meant I'd have to wait for the one that would leave the next day. My permit was for twenty-four hours only and I would officially be a deserter by the morning. This was dangerous because the Croatian police was known for random ID checks and I was fucked if I got caught. But there was no turning back for me, I can tell you, this was it, my golden opportunity. So I slept in the car at the harbour car park and in the morning I ran to the newsagents to get some cigarettes and something to eat just before the ferry left.

'I was walking towards the ferry when I saw two policemen walking around. I started to run and as soon as I stepped onto the ferry its stepping board lifted up and it edged away at the last minute. The policemen were looking over at the ferry, but I suppose they weren't sure if I'd ran just to catch the ferry, which was leaving, or if I was a suspicious character, and they carried on walking. And I suppose they just couldn't be bothered to cause all the fuss of stopping the ferry and all that.

'The island was deserted. We docked and I remembered how back before the war old ladies would swarm around the harbour offering rooms, whispering "rooms,

rooms, rooms" into your ear like witchcraft, and buzzing around the tourists like spell-making bees. Now there was nothing, hardly any sound at all, not even the crickets, it was still too cold for them. The air, the sky, the sea, everything was still and instead of noise penetrating my senses, I was overwhelmed by the smell of pines. It was the first sense of peace and silence I'd felt for over a year, and the first moment I was relaxed enough to enjoy nature since the beginning of the war.

'Me and the three other ferry passengers walked onto the gravelly path and I asked a woman where the house of Mr Brkić was. She pointed to a white house nearby, without speaking. I thanked her and she nodded. I was so paranoid of everyone, even the mute lady in the middle of an island with a population of three. I walked quickly to the house, just to get off the street. I knocked and an old woman appeared.

'"Is this the house of Mr Brkić?"

'"Who are you and what do you want?" She had a moustache and a wart on her chin.

'"I am Zlatko and I called a couple of days ago. I'm here for business. Mr Brkić knows I'm coming."

'I tried to sound as if I knew what I was talking about. I pronounced the word "business" with importance and it seemed to do the trick because she let me into the dark sitting room.

'"He's away until tomorrow morning. You will sleep

here tonight and you will probably leave tomorrow night."

'I spent the day there at the Brkić household eating and sleeping. The old grandma softened up and told me some village stories. She lived there alone with her son, Mr Brkić. I had no idea what kind of a character he was, but he was certainly making a lot of cash out of this. I was paying him all the money I had plus what I'd borrowed off my uncle. I slept badly that night, and my stomach felt like solid lead. At dawn I heard Mr Brkić enter the house and say: "Good morning, mama" and the clanking of the dishes from the kitchen. I got up and went downstairs and he told me that we would leave that night and that he had no papers for me, but that I would cross the borders in the boot of his car. But as he said that, he looked me up and down and said: "Fucking hell, I hope you're gonna fit!" and added: "You'll be all right, last month I had two people in that boot. A bit cramped, but they survived." He laughed. "What if they search the car at the border?" I asked. "Leave that to me," he said.

'I've no idea how he gets past the border guards. Maybe he has some arrangement with them, who knows. But we drove, and every time we approached a border, I would get into the boot until we crossed. Sometimes it took an hour, two, three. There would be voices, shouts, whispers, silence. Inside the boot it was dark, and two small holes let in stinky exhaust air and rays of dusty light. He'd drilled the holes himself with his new Black and Decker drill that he'd bought off the money he'd earned transporting people across borders. I was cramped, my knees against my chin, and I only had a couple of inches to move each way. I was lying there trying to sleep, not to think of the claustrophobia gripping me, trying not to compare which is better: war or this? Trench or car boot? Then, he would stop, open the boot, I'd go blind instantaneously from the light, breathe lots of panicked breaths, and get back into the car. Every time I was in the boot, all I could think of was that stupid song "Get out of my dreams, get into my car". I don't even like that song.

'We drove like that for three days and out of the seventy-two-hour journey, I spent fifteen in the boot. When he put me on a ferry from Rotterdam to Hull, he said: "You're on your own now." He was all right, Mr Brkić. A kind of an island guy, quiet, skin like a raisin, a big moustache. I asked him why he did what he did and he said: "Well, it pays good money and it's for a good cause." He was a fisherman before the war, but he and his mother found it hard to survive on the money he got selling fish in Split. I asked him how often he had to drive people across the border and he said twice a month on average. But he wouldn't tell me how he got past the guards. Or if anyone had ever suffocated in the boot when the border wait took too long.

'Get out of my dreams, get into my car'

'So when I got to the immigration point in Hull, I declared: "I am from Bosnia and I am seeking asylum." That's what he said I should do. They took me into a room, questioned me for hours and I filled out forms and forms. They said that I could get accommodation while my application was being processed, so I'm staying in this bed and breakfast place. It's all right.'

After that Zlatko stayed with us for a couple of months in the spring, until he decided to move to London and look for work there. Sometimes at night, as he fell asleep on our sofa, we'd hear him humming 'Get out of my dreams, get into my car'.

How they won the lottery

Refugees don't often get rich overnight.

The K family lived next door to us in Hull. Their daughter Maya and I worked together in a take-away for a few pounds an hour; I washed the dishes and she prepared barbecue ribs and pork chops. In 1995, three years after arriving in the UK, her family bought a dog, at Maya's insistence. I went round to see the puppy, a soft little thing with a doughy belly. Maya was to look after the dog completely, said her father, 'not like with everything else, fun for the first few months, and then hop! here you are mother and father, you look after it! No way Jose!' Mr K said 'No way Jose' in English and wagged his finger in her face. He'd just learned that phrase.

Maya was happy. She had her Labrador puppy, like the one she'd seen in the Andrex toilet paper advert. She tried to get her own dog to pull the loo roll, but the puppy would just chew the paper and make a mess. A different kind of mess, a lot less charming than the ad – especially when her mother saw it.

'I knew this dog was going to be trouble! Why did you ever buy it for her? Now I have to pick up pieces of wet toilet paper around the house! Bloody hell! In Bosnia, a dog is a dog – it lives outside, like all bloody animals. A house is for a human. In this country you've gone mad, both of you. Soon, the dog will be more important than your own mother!' My mother used to say the same thing about the cat we had briefly before the war. We had to get rid of it when its February mating season came because it started howling from the balcony and waking all our neighbours.

But Maya and her father loved the dog and took him out for walks every day, rambled around the park until the golden puppy was so tired they had to carry him home. Sometimes I came along too, running with the dog. His name was Pero, and we'd come up with it together – it was a play on *perro*, the Spanish word for dog, and an old-fashioned Yugoslav name. I loved Pero's warm little body, his heart beating fast, and his soft bloated belly rising up and down with each breath. Maya sometimes put a mirror under his wet nose when he slept, to check he was still breathing. Her mother secretly watched her and remembered herself doing the same with Maya when she was only a few days old.

Bluebird

During their walks, Maya and her father always played the lottery. I never joined them in this, because I thought the lottery was condescending, with its myth that your problems would disappear with a million pounds. I was also afraid that if I won, I'd use up all my life's luck in one move. Maya's father said that he'd rather have money than luck, and perhaps he was right. Luck is a relative thing; but then again, so is money. Mr K always played a set of the same, twenty-year-old numbers, the numbers he'd played back home; Maya always chose at random. She tried to get her father to play different numbers, these ones obviously not being particularly lucky, but he refused on the grounds that if he changed now and these numbers came up and won the jackpot at some point in the future, he would kill himself. Maya thought this a bit extreme, but understood her father's reasoning, feeling sorry for the unfortunate situation he was in. It didn't help that he refused to play more than one combination of numbers a week, so he couldn't even 'cheat' on his usual numbers with a different, perhaps more fortunate, set. This week, as her father marked his choices automatically, Maya looked around the shop. She spotted £1.99 on a price tag for fig biscuits. She liked fig biscuits and marked number 19. Similarly, she saw 1000 on a vitamin C box and thought that vitamin C was a good thing, so marked number 10. Maya's puppy was resting on the lottery counter, looking out of the window with sleepy eyes, and her gaze fell on his chequered collar that she'd bought the day before. On it hung a silver pendant with his registration number engraved, in case he was, God forbid, lost. She copied the registration number on to her lottery card. And they went home.

She was excited about the lottery, but had to go to work in the evening and missed the show where the lottery balls fall into the transparent plastic tube, revealing the winning numbers. She told me that she'd played that day, and on our break we made ridiculous lists of what she'd do with the money if she won. She did this every Saturday night on our break and I partook in her fantasy lists happily. Big houses with swimming pools and private jets featured prominently. At midnight, after she'd placed the white card lid into the corners of the last aluminium food container and wrapped the silver corners around the round edges of the lid, she washed her hands and hung up her apron, ready to go home. I took off my thick rubber gloves that still glistened with soap and we left the grim kitchen together. Tired, we discussed whether we could get away with leaving our hair unwashed until the following day, despite not liking to go to sleep smelling of fried oil and rib sauce. She wondered if the smell was only buried deeply in her nostrils, or whether her hair really did stink. And discussing these take-away concerns, we stepped off the 23 bus. We walked the eight steps to Maya's door and said goodbye. I carried on a little further as Maya opened her front door and Pero came to greet her, wagging his tail wildly and shoving his small muzzle into her shoes. I saw her pick him up gently and let him lick her face for a moment, and I briefly craved a puppy of my own. I knew I wasn't a natural pet keeper and settled for Pero's proximity as a surrogate cuddly thing.

I came home and sat down in front of the TV. This was my after-work routine, the time to relax, to check the news. I knew that Maya did the same, only she checked her lottery numbers first. She later told me that her father had come downstairs and said: 'Let's see if we're millionaires.' So they checked: 10 on the ticket – 10 on the TV; 19 on the ticket – 19 on the TV; 7 on the ticket – 7 on the TV. And so on until they reached the last number, and all the numbers matched.

'Dad, they are all matching,' Maya said.

'Let me see that,' said her father and grabbed the lottery ticket from her hand. 'Don't piss about.'

Mr K compared the numbers at least ten times before he let out a squeal so high-pitched that he frightened Pero. At this point, Maya phoned me and said: 'Come over right now, and hurry up.' I walked over to their house, thinking they were going to tell me someone had died. I found them hopping around the living room, yelling: 'We are millionaires! Refugee fucking millionaires!'

How they won the lottery

After that, Maya left the take-away. They bought a modest house in London, a place with a garden where Pero could run around, and moved close to where their relatives lived. They kept their win a secret. She went to a good school, and we occasionally wrote to each other. I told Maya I missed her when I washed up, and I filled her in on Hull gossip. She told me that Mr K had bought himself a sailing boat and white driving gloves that he said reminded him of President Tito's. Mrs K invested in shares and diamond rings that she never wore for fear of being robbed; she was also worried that her friends might get suspicious.

As for me, I still don't play the lottery.

Bound

Everyone travelled during the summer and at Christmas. Everyone, that is, except for me. And the other refugees, of course. My passport, small and grey – the colour of minors' passports – lay uselessly in its expired Yugoslavness, buried under dusty papers and application forms, and ignored by officials at Croydon's Lunar House, the main Home Office building. As my international friends trickled away to see their parents or laze on a Mediterranean or Far Eastern beach, I tried to remember my passport: it had my thirteen-year-old face embedded on the photo, and the address where I'd spent most of my life now felt so far away it might as well never have existed. My father's signature sat like a knot on the bottom of the page. Everything on that passport was useless, changed, or altogether gone.

*

Bound

As a child, I was wild about my bicycle. I used to go on long rides, kilometres out of town, cycling along the river, all the way to a lake where I could have a swim. My mother never knew that I went so far on my own, or that I cycled on the main road, until one day I got a puncture and I had to call home. 'Promise not to be angry if I tell you something,' I told my mother. She promised. 'I've had a puncture.' 'Oh, OK,' she said. 'Where are you?' 'I'm by the river, on the lake.' 'On the lake?!!' she shouted. 'You're angry,' I said. 'Of course I'm bloody angry! You're cycling on the main road! You could get killed!' My father came to pick me up and we sealed the puncture at home, in the bathroom basin; we submerged the rubber tube in water and looked for bubbles that indicated the punctured spot.

In Hull, I'd resorted to hitchhiking or getting lifts with friends, and I also tried to save money for buses or trains. I couldn't leave the country, so I travelled around the UK, feeling like the steel ball inside a pinball machine, moving up and down the ingrained passageways, but never bolting out of bounds.

A French friend and I hitchhiked to the Lake District. Paranoid about getting picked up by a homicidal lunatic, we each carried a bottle of anti-perspirant deodorant in our handbags that we planned to spray in the eyes of an imaginary attacker, as well as on our armpits. Luckily, we were always picked up by kindly people. I remembered a story from a letter my mother had sent a month before. She was going from Mostar to my grandmother's village, which was only a twenty-minute drive away and most people passed it on their way out of town. My mother didn't have a car and the bus was very late, so she put out her hand when she saw a car coming. It stopped, a large 4×4 that was unusually glitzy for Mostar at the time. She looked in and saw one of the biggest local warlords sitting behind the wheel, grinning. She didn't want to get into his car so she started making excuses, saying that she wasn't waving to get him to stop, that she was just stretching her arms. She swears it was the only excuse she could think of at the time. The man didn't make a fuss; he just drove off.

I went to visit a friend in Wolverhampton, a town so dreary that it made Hull appear an aesthetic haven.

Then I saved some money and went to see a Bosnian girl, Lila, whom I'd met a few months before and who had immediately become one of my best friends. Lila and I used to buy cheap cigarettes at Tesco's discount counter; I can't remember the brand, but they were long, thin and black – like something from a 1980s film. Half the cigarettes in the packet were always broken (which is why they were cheaper), and we wrapped white roll-up papers around each one, like a bandage. This spoilt the air of sophisticated elegance we were aiming for. Lila and

Bound

I travelled to London and around the city on buses and trains, sometimes buying a train ticket, other times hiding in the toilets until our stop. We went to Brighton and sat on the beach, eating crab and chips bought in the small seaside kiosks. We hitchhiked to Whitstable and dreamed of owning one of the hundreds of tiny beach huts that sat, varicoloured, on the windy beach.

On a visit to London, Lila and I sheltered from the rain in Covent Garden Piazza. Next to us was a tall ginger-haired boy, our age, wearing a T-shirt that read 'I Am the Walrus'. Lila said she liked him, so we approached him with our black and white bandaged cigarettes, asking for a light. We commented on the weather. 'We're Lila and Vesna,' we said and shook his hand. 'I'm Michael,' he said in an American accent. We chatted under the dripping eaves until the rain stopped, and then went for coffee. Michael was on his gap year – a concept entirely unfamiliar to me – and had very little in his bag, save for an all-purpose bottle of soap that served as shampoo, body wash, clothes wash and washing-up liquid. We spent that entire night in the 100 Club on Oxford Street, where my friend Nenad worked as a cleaner. The club was empty apart from Nenad, who mopped the floor while Lila and Michael flirted and tinkled on the piano and I played someone's records, stacked up behind the bar.

I went to Birmingham, Leeds, Newcastle, Bath, Bristol and several small towns whose names I can't remember any more, with my friend Salvatore, whose job involved travelling around England promoting pharmaceutical products. He was good company. We sang on the way between his business calls, and I wandered round the towns until he finished his meetings. I'd look for a nice place to eat, and we'd go for dinner there before driving back up to Hull. It felt good to move, to be bound for somewhere.

Spice

I quit the take-away after a few months. I hated the smell of grease that wafted from the blackened pans and the sadness of barbecue sauce on an arched rib at the bottom of a squeaky aluminium container. I'd managed to get the job of my dreams: I became a clerk in a video shop called Spice. Spice wasn't just any video shop – it stocked world cinema, movies by big and small independent directors, French classics, people I'd never heard of. I was going to get paid very little, but I couldn't wait to start.

I landed the job thanks to Sebastian, my sister's boy-friend, who was a prolific dope smoker. Sebastian, my sister and I were all film enthusiasts and we'd just registered as customers at Spice, when Sebastian got into conversation with Archie, the owner, about some special type of grass that Archie enjoyed smoking. I have no idea how the two men came to this subject in the first place, but minutes later Archie and Sebastian were at the back of the shop getting stoned, while I sat watching them – my brain was too weak and inflexible to cope with drugs. I asked Archie if they needed anyone to help at the shop and he said: 'Well yes, actually, we do.' I started the following day.

Spice was quite small, with a makeshift counter, a computer and a TV suspended on a corner wall. It was almost always quiet and I watched films by Krzysztof Kieślowski, Hall Hartley, Zhang Yimou, Truffaut, Godard (which I never understood), John Cassavetes and countless others; when my shifts were over, I turned off the lights, locked up and stayed behind the counter, gawping up at the suspended TV screen. I felt as if I'd discovered an entire new universe and imagined living inside a movie, like Mia Farrow in *Purple Rose of Cairo*.

There were also some books and comics, and I learned about Robert Crumb, and read Kerouac and Ginsberg for the first time. Archie had great taste in films and books, but he told too many dirty jokes, and his sideways glances were unsettling.

A man called George co-owned Spice and shared a house with Archie. George was a gentle soul, with large glasses. He suffered from a muscle-wasting disease that had confined him to a wheelchair. He kept a baseball bat under the counter, which he said I was to use if I needed to in self-defence. I wielded it once when a group of local

Spice

adolescents tried to rob the shop and they ran away. I
have no idea what would have happened had they not
done so.

The customers were mainly local art students and,
after recommending a film, I ended up dating a few.
There was Zoltan, a graphic designer of Hungarian
descent who was by turns jealous and generous, and
whose dark and melancholy moods I found difficult to
bear. I flirted with an art teacher who carried his Jack
Russell on a cushion inside his bicycle basket when he
came to take out videos every Sunday. Then there was
Jim, a tall trumpeter who could have been famous had he
not dropped out of his later-successful band. Jim had a
caricature face, a hairy chest and liked to surprise me
when I was returning home by jumping out of the bushes
outside my house. We laughed a lot when we were
together and I enjoyed going to the weekly open mic
night in a local bar, where Jim played three-second trum-
pet pieces, followed by a parade of Fellini-esque
characters who thought they possessed stage presence.
After Jim left Hull to pursue his trumpeting career I was
wooed by Paul. Paul was a former car hijacker who once
climbed on to my second-floor window sill in the middle
of the night, drunk and shouting 'England lost!' (It took
me months to recover from the fright.) He also proposed
to take me to Whitby on Valentine's Day in a stolen vehicle, but I gave him a firm no.

Bluebird

A few times that year, Lila came up, and we sat around Spice for hours, watching films and chatting to customers. We rode bicycles – like everyone in town – and I became an expert at buying bicycles no one would want to steal. This meant I ended up riding a bike with no brakes, and I'd have to put both my feet on the sides of the front wheel when I wanted to stop. Someone once tried stealing that bike, but left it leaning against the side of the wall some forty metres down the road.

At night, we went to Spiders, a club at the edge of town that sold vodka shots for 50p and pints of beer for £1. All of Hull's students congregated at Spiders, alongside the club's original Goth crowd. The music was terrible, the fake cobweb-filled interior hideous, but no one cared. Cycling home at dawn, as darkness was blotted out of the sky, I was truly happy. I was twenty years old and doing A-levels at Hull College. My status was not yet resolved, and if I was not declared a refugee, I would have to pay enormous fees if I wanted to study at university. But I wasn't in a hurry. I thought that my real learning was happening right then and there, in Hull.

All in all, Spice existed for only about a year. After the first six months of the shop's short life, Archie started going out with a fragile Norwegian beauty called Alice. I made friends with her, and she used to tell me about her twin sister, who lived back in Norway. Alice taught Norwegian in Hull, while her sister, Annie, taught

Norwegian in a school in Norway. According to Alice, the two sisters always wanted to do the same thing, but there weren't enough jobs in their small town, so Alice decided to try an entirely new country and came to England. After some time, she moved in with Archie. She came to Spice one day and as she lifted her arm to point at something, I caught a glimpse of a plum bruise above her elbow. I asked her what had happened to her, and she said: 'Oh, I fell down the stairs.' A few weeks later, she had a contusion the shape of Africa on her cheek and George said that Archie was beating her; he'd first heard it from his bedroom, and then saw it one evening. George had talked to Archie – who apparently experienced rage when he was drunk, and extreme shame when he was sober – and told him to stop. He had even threatened to call the police if it happened again, and Archie had apparently agreed to stop hitting his girlfriend. The subsequent beatings, George said, went on when he was out. The next day, I went along to Alice and Archie's house with a couple of female friends. We took Alice out for a coffee and told her we knew about the abuse. I wasn't sure whether what we were doing was right or whether we were intruding into what was none of our business; after all, Archie was my employer. Alice burst into tears and told us to ring her sister. Annie booked a plane ticket to Norway, and a few days later, Alice left Hull for ever.

The day Alice ran away, Archie came into Spice,

frantically shouting: 'Where is she?' I was shelving videos and George was going through the books. After our talk, I wasn't sure if Alice would really leave, but I was glad to hear that her resolve hadn't weakened. 'We all know that you were beating her, Archie,' I said. After a prolonged silence during which I carried on tidying the already tidy shelves and George scribbled, Archie sat down on one of the chairs usually reserved for browsing customers and started sobbing. George said: 'The business is broke,' took some money out of the till and went to the pub. Archie followed him.

He came into the shop the next morning and said he knew he'd done a terrible thing but that he loved Alice. Apparently, he had called her sister in Norway the night before and had spoken to Alice. She was angry and told him she didn't want to see him again, but he apologised many times and she relented a little. I said: 'I'd never forgive you if it were me, but then again, I'd never go out with you, and if you – or any man – ever tried to hit me, I'd kill you in your sleep.' I said it calmly but Archie was weeping again. Customers walked into the shop but left hurriedly. After he went home that day I never saw him again.

The next day, Archie took all of his and George's money (they'd apparently put some aside to pay off some of their debts) and went to Norway. He sneaked out in the middle of the night, leaving a note to George that read: 'Sorry, I had to leave, I love Alice. PS. I took the money, sorry, Archie.' Alice sent me a card some months later, saying she was happy with Archie in Norway, that things had changed. Soon after, Spice closed down. We took down the shelves and packed the videos in cardboard boxes. Outside, the wind carried stray leaflets that offered '2 for 1' video deals.

The beauty queen

I'd put my name down as an interpreter in Hull's refugee office and one morning I got a call to come in; a new convoy had arrived from Bosnia. I was to translate for Anka, an elderly woman who had just come to Hull across the North Sea on a ferry from Holland. The convoy had left Bosnia five days before and the journey, capped by a night on unsteady waters, had left everyone dizzy and exhausted. There were another few volunteer translators and we listened to terrible stories of disappearances, murder and torture – many of these people had come from the area surrounding Srebrenica. Anka had travelled alone. She had been in a refugee camp for six months before leaving the country. Her voice was small and she sat hunched over on the chair, staring at a steaming teacup in front of her as she spoke.

'The tents stretched across the once green fields for

miles. The patches of grass were interrupted with small mud puddles or dust, depending on the weather. We were ten to a tent, men and women separated, the women with the children.

'In the summer the heat became stifling under the nylon covers, and in winter we slept in huddles to keep warm. Every morning different people from the camp brought bread and hot coffee for breakfast. In the evening, we queued for a dinner of soup and vegetables or macaroni and cheese. I shared a tent with a family of nine. I had nobody, so the camp organisers put us together. We came to regard each other as family. They went to Sweden before me, part of a family convoy.

'You see, I was the beauty queen of my village in 1950, five years after the Second World War, when everyone was poor but happy. There was optimism then. After this war, there will be nothing but misery. We had ideals then, we fought for something, against something. We were united. We had a leader and there seemed to be some future. I was taught to write and read, and I could get a job. But I preferred to earn my money winning beauty contests.'

If you squinted really hard so your eyelids trembled, you could picture Anka's former beauty. She still had long hair and used lipstick. You didn't need to try to imagine her youthful looks because she had with her a small notebook containing photos and cuttings from her local newspaper. She stood proudly, a blond beehive on her head, eyes painted, lips pouting. The bathing suit she wore was one of those modest 1950s one-piece affairs, and the pale leg closest to the camera was always lightly bent.

'I couldn't believe it when they came to my house, those young boys, with weapons and in army uniforms. I never thought anyone was going to disturb me, I was famous in the village. Everyone knew my name: Anka Vulic, and where I lived. So when they knocked on the door so loudly and said: "Anka open the door!" I was a bit annoyed, you know. "Who is that, so rude?" I thought. Before I answered the door, I looked through the peep-hole and I saw these two boys, and I recognized one of them, he was the son of the butcher down the road. I didn't open the door completely, I had the chain on and I said: "What do you want boys?" And that's when they broke the door down. I was so scared I could hardly breathe.'

She started to cry and I comforted her.

'When they came in I asked them again what they wanted and they just went around my house and smashed everything. "Gold Anka, gold is what we want," they said and carried on smashing the dishes in my vitrine, the china I'd bought in Moscow years ago, in 1973; they toppled my coffee tables and searched through my jewellery boxes. They took all my jewellery.

The beauty queen

Two boys, with guns, just like that. My neighbours had said days before: "Anka, you have to go and live with your daughter, you can't be alone in times like these." But I refused. I thought that everyone knew me, that no one would hurt an old woman like me. But this was a new generation. I took my picture of Jesus off the wall and hid it underneath my dressing gown. It was my mother's, that picture, the only thing in the house I cared about. And I rescued it.'

I later discovered that she kept her picture of Jesus, tattered, torn, one of his eyes scratched out, under her pillow the way criminals keep guns, and she prayed to it every night before she went to sleep.

'Those boys, they were beasts. I knew one of them, I told you, his father was a butcher and before the war I used to buy my meat in his shop. Then another butcher opened down the same street. It was a better shop, the floors were clean, the man was polite and smiling, and he somehow seemed to give you more meat per kilo than old Branko. Branko's shop was full of flies and the smell wasn't so good, and he was always sweating and wiping his brow with the edge of his blood-sprinkled apron. It wasn't so nice, no. This new man was a Slovenian and you know what they are like, something like Germans, meticulous, his apron was spotless every day and he never seemed to get blood on it. So everyone started shopping for meat at the Slovene's and old Branko went out of business. He had some loyal customers left, like his drinking mates, but they never had money and he gave them lamb chops and chicken wings on credit. So old Branko started to stand outside his shop, with carcasses hanging on hooks behind him, reeking terribly, and shouting: "You'll see you bastards, I'll show you all one day who old Branko is, I'll show you I'm a fine butcher." And things like that. Everyone thought he'd gone mad. Even the drunkards stopped coming to the shop, they couldn't stand the smell. When the first shelling started old Branko went out in the street with his big meat cleavers, screaming: "My time has come, I'm gonna cut you all up for my shop!" But before he could harm anyone, a shell landed nearby and killed him. I thought his son was probably crazy from all that mess with his father.

'So that day they stole all my jewellery and what they didn't steal they broke. When they were leaving they said: "Don't cry grandma, you're lucky we didn't slit your throat, but we might next time." And they laughed when they said that, and felt nothing for me, crying, old and frightened. That night I was lying stiff in my bed, my picture of Jesus under my dressing gown, hoping those boys wouldn't come back. I sent a message via some friends to my daughter to tell her what had happened, but it was already getting dark and no one could go anywhere during the curfew. She came first thing in the morning.

She'd heard that old Branko's son was raiding houses and stealing, and there was a lot of looting in the village. There was probably nothing left to steal in the shops any more, so they went to people's houses, she said. That's when she sent me to the camp. She didn't want to leave the village, her husband was in the army and she didn't want to leave him alone. I wish I could go back to my village to see them again. To be in my home.'

Anka wept and wept.

After that I visited her every week for a few months in her home in Hull. Whenever I went round, if she was upset or lonely and crying, I would ask: 'Show me the pictures when you were a Miss, come on; tell me about your first competition, when you won that little dog on a leash.' I would open the notebook on the photo of her as an eighteen-year-old beauty with a small dog in her arms, and she would start retelling me the story, her sobs slowing down.

A refugee, at last

My sister had been granted refugee status and left for
Italy on a student exchange programme, where she was
to stay for the entire year. Her boyfriend returned to
Croatia and I moved to a one-bedroom attic flat in an old
building that leaned sideways like the tower of Pisa. A DJ
friend had lived there before and left rows of records
behind, though I could never play a single one because I
didn't have a record player. I painted the walls 'Cornfield'
and 'Azure', and rested my coffee cups on a swinging
table in the living room, suspended from the sloping ceiling and made by the DJ. I listened to a lot of Laurie
Anderson at the time, and enjoyed her silly lyrics, such as:
'The sun is like a big bald head' or 'It's a sky-blue sky'. I
also had a cat, a fat white thing, that I was partly looking
after and partly borrowing from a peregrinating friend
because I thought I'd heard the rustling of mice in my

bedroom. The cat was sweet though it occasionally had uncontrollable fits of energy, when it shot from the Azure living room to the Cornfield kitchen like an insane bullet.

I loved sitting in front of the gas fire late at night, with a blanket over my knees and the cat on the blanket. I sat there, reading or listening to Laurie Anderson. Friends were always coming round and, although I had very little money, I was happy. The only problem was that I was in my final year of A-levels and I'd applied to various universities, but still had heard nothing from the Home Office for what was now getting on to be the fourth year. I was worried I would not be able to start a degree the coming September. A friend advised me to ask for help from my local MP.

The first time I visited the MP, I wore a Lenin badge. I wore the badge like most people wear a Che Guevara or Chairman Mao T-shirt, as a decorative, or 'cool' thing, though I was, of course, raised to respect Comrade Lenin's work and ideas. The MP's office was surprisingly ordinary: a desk was covered in papers, with more papers in stacks on its corners, like columns. Family photographs and diplomas hung on the wall. I'd expected a British government office to look more majestic, with gilded furniture and photos of the Queen or at least John Major. Back home, the country's leader's photo was on the wall of every office.

The MP was a rotund middle-aged man, who greeted

me politely and asked me how he could help. I could see him eyeing my Lenin badge. I knew he was a Labour MP, and I thought his gaze at the vitreous red badge, where Lenin's profile was illuminated by the daylight, was of admiration. I told him about my status hold-up and explained my anxiety regarding my university applications, and I asked him to write to the Home Office and enquire about my case. He said he'd be glad to help and promised results within a few months. I was encouraged by the meeting and as I was leaving we shook hands and I asked him if he liked my badge. I wanted to give it to him, as thanks for helping me. The MP shook his head and said: 'I don't know how you can support this man when he was responsible for so much oppression and murder.' I didn't know what he was talking about. Lenin's words had echoed throughout my primary education, his quote 'To learn, to learn, and only to learn' imprinted on the first page of each of our text books. The next time I went to see the MP, I didn't wear the badge.

Around the same time, I started working in a small restaurant called Bonnie's, in Hull's old town, the only part of the city that had survived the Blitz. It was an area of cobblestone streets bordered by Victorian and Georgian houses, but it felt like an oasis of quaintness amid the army of faceless post-war terraces that covered the rest of the city. I imagined that looked at from above Hull would resemble a picture on a tattered jigsaw puzzle, faded except for a burst of colour in the middle, where the old town stood.

I was the washing-up girl at Bonnie's. I shared the kitchen with the owner, Brian, who was also the chef, and a German girl, Katrin, who, despite being a kitchen assistant and therefore technically a notch up from a washing-up girl in the restaurant hierarchy, competed furiously with me. If I was cleaning the work surfaces at the end of the night, she'd be scouring the stove and the oven, and getting under the cupboards to hard-to-reach places. I'd then decide we needed to clean all the obscure parts of the kitchen, and we would soon be scrubbing every corner of the restaurant. Brian wondered how he got such diligent workers! One day a friend of mine who was friendly with a friend of Katrin's (the usual intricate paths for the circulation of gossip), told me that Katrin thought I was interested in her boyfriend, Mick, because I always asked: 'How is Mick?' when I saw her. The truth is that I couldn't think of anything else to say because she made me feel uncomfortable. Now I understood that she was always competing with me because she thought I fancied her man. So from then on, I just asked: 'How are you?' when I met Katrin.

In fact I had a serious crush on Brian, the owner of Bonnie's, who was unbearably faithful to his absentee girlfriend, away travelling the world for a year. He was tall, with curly, unruly hair and a gentle face; he wore thick cardigans, which only enhanced his appeal in my eyes. I liked everything about him: the way he smoked, talked and joked; the way he chopped, fried, boiled and poached. He sang as he cooked, and I wanted his cheerfulness around me all the time and not just as I stood over a steaming sink. He had a selection of 'The Worst Songs in the World' which he sometimes played in the restaurant and which I adored. At the end of the night, all the restaurant workers went to Brian's house, or to Spiders, and stayed up until sunrise. Every morning I went to sleep dreaming of Brian and how happy we might be together, 'The Worst Songs in the World' the soundtrack to our life. But I knew that the path between me and Brian was filled not only with a large obstacle, in the shape of his girlfriend, but also with the fact that he hadn't an iota of amorous interest in me.

Years later, when I was no longer living in Hull but went back to visit, I met Brian in the street. As we chatted, a bunch of magazines fell from his bag and on to the pavement. I bent to pick them up and saw a woman masturbating on the front page, a big red nail on her finger. I looked at Brian, who rapidly stepped on the magazine with his black suede shoe. We both felt uncomfortable and made excuses for having to leave in opposite directions.

After many washed and dried plates at Bonnie's and several letters from my MP to the Home Office, I received an envelope that carried the emblem of the immigration department. It was autumn 1996, and the cat was leaving its fur all over the flat, shedding its summer coat. I was on the verge of developing an obsessive-compulsive vacuuming disorder, but nothing helped. The morning the letter arrived, the sound of the doorbell blended in with the sound of the vacuum cleaner, but the postman rang furiously. I ran downstairs and when I opened the door, he was leaning on the bell and tongue-tossing a toothpick in his mouth. 'Yes?' I said. 'Miss Maric?' He smiled; he had an accent that I took to be Polish, and he pronounced my surname properly, 'Marich'. 'That's me,' I said, and he handed me the envelope. 'From Her Majesty, the Queen!' he said and produced a piece of paper on which I wrote my name and then signed. 'Have a nice day!' he called out and I thanked him.

I carried the letter up the stairs as if it were a living thing, careful not to damage it in any way. I entered the flat, made a coffee and sat on my sofa. The smoke of the cigarette spiralled upwards and the letter sat on the suspended coffee table, still innocent in its white envelope. I put the cat on the sofa next to me; I wanted to savour the last few moments of my life as it was then, because whatever decision the letter carried, things were going to change. The universities I'd applied to were in London and Glasgow, though if my asylum application was rejected, I would have to go back to Bosnia. Despite my homesickness and the loneliness that I'd battled with over the years, the idea of living in Bosnia again frightened me. The cat sat beside me calmly. I stroked its head, took a drag on the cigarette, sipped the coffee and opened the envelope. The letter read:

> Dear Miss Maric,
>
> We are pleased to inform you that your refugee status has been granted as of September 1996, for the duration of four years. After the initial four years, you will be entitled to apply to be naturalised, and become a British citizen.

I read the letter again, kissed it and shrieked, which frightened the cat. I flew down the stairs and into the street, to one of Hull's white phone boxes, and dialled my mother's number. 'Mum, it's me,' I said. 'I am a refugee, at last.'

I was entitled to a travel document, which I immediately applied for. A few weeks later, I was notified that it was ready for collection. The Hull immigration office was a small concrete building close to the port that I knew from my few interpreting jobs, and every time I neared it, through the worn-out industrial landscape that slumped on the edge of the sea, I thanked God that it wasn't my first memory of Britain. I went in, signed and was given a brown envelope. Inside was a booklet the same shape and size as a regular passport, its navy front cover printed with:

Titre de Voyage
Travel Document
1951 United Nations Convention Relating to
the Status of Refugees

There were two black stripes in the upper right corner, signifying something, though I never learned what. On the last page was my photo, name, place of birth and country of residence. The document stated that British embassies weren't responsible for help or assistance while I was abroad and I wondered whether Bosnia and Herzegovina had any embassies – it was struggling to set up a government – and who would help me if I was in trouble. I entered a travel agency where strip lighting illuminated photos of exotic destinations. My heart beat fast as an assistant waved me over to her desk. I was going home.

Coming home

The first time you go back to your country, it's autumn 1996 and the war has been over for more than a year, though there are still incidents, bombs, occasional explosions. You are living in Hull, a city that will in the future be voted the worst place to live in on some 'crapathon' and everyone will tell you about it, even though you haven't lived there for years. But you like it. You have your own small flat, in the attic of an old house, a little haven you still dream of sometimes when you want to be left alone. The day you leave, you stuff your backpack tight, full of clothes, towels, books.

That day your two good friends arrive and bring you a bunch of roses to throw from the ferry you are travelling on, for good luck. One of them advises you to drink a tablespoon of oil, also for good luck, which you wisely decline. The two boys take your bag, put it in a taxi, give you a loud kiss on each cheek and close the cab door with a slam. An overwhelming sense of liberation and fear is brewing inside you. The journey will last a long time, because it is the only way you can afford it. A ferry will take you from Hull to Rotterdam (fourteen hours), and then a coach will knit the journey from Amsterdam to Split (twenty-eight hours), followed by a slow and smelly bus crawling from Split to Mostar (four hours). In total, forty-six hours on the move, time which suits you just fine, time you will use to shed your anglicized skin and get used to 'continental ways' once again.

You get out of the cab, put your backpack on your shoulders, and nearly fall over. The fact that your friend carried it to the taxi from the flat means that you had no idea how heavy it was when you could still do something about it. It is like putting an overweight teenager on your back, you think. You are not sure that you will be able to carry such a burdensome bag and consider discarding some items, when you notice the sign 'DO NOT THROW ANYTHING OVERBOARD'. Suddenly you feel that perhaps the ferry can read your mind and wonder if you can throw the bunch of roses in the sea, like your friend has told you to do, because you are starting to find them annoying. You seek out a quiet spot and hurl the flowers into the water, quickly and surreptitiously like a criminal, not with the poignancy and grand gesture that you had imagined, celebrating your freedom, you think.

Bluebird

You go and find a place you can leave your bag, and a nice boy with curly hair helps you with it, remarking on its weight. Your shoulders hurt and your back feels tight, like when you come home after you've been washing up for five hours, standing up in the restaurant kitchen.

You and the curly-haired boy go out on to the deck and smoke a cigarette. Then you explore the ferry alone, finding things you are surprised anyone would put on a ferry, such as a disco mirror-ball, a karaoke and fruit machines. The 'social area' resembles a bad northern pub, which is perhaps what it's trying to resemble, you think. In the 'buffet area' they sell fish and chips, sausages and other stuff you don't want to eat. The food is displayed in an oily glass case, heated from below, the sausages pressed against the glass like a greasy face. It's getting dark and you watch the sky change colour over the sea as you sail past places like Grimsby, Goole, Gilberdyke and other small towns with depressing Nordic names. You sit and listen to music and write things down in your diary and feel happy that you are moving, for this is what you really love – being on the move. It is especially good that you are alone to enjoy the feeling without having to make any kind of conversation with anyone.

When it's time to go to sleep it's dark and the ferry is bobbing. They say the sea is 'a bit rough' tonight. You sit on your chair in the dark, concentrating on mind-controlling your seasickness. Just when you think you are succeeding, a group of drunk young men come into the sleeping room, talking loudly, breaking your concentration and waking everybody up. You decide that you might as well vomit all over them, since they are annoying you. Their seats are next to yours and they start saying things like: 'Oi mate, no one told me there's a beauty sitting next to me.' You feel a mixture of flattery and fear, and pretend you are fast asleep. Thankfully, they don't talk to you, each other or at all after that and fall asleep quickly. And so do you.

In the morning, the curly-haired boy helps you with your bag again. He is kind and you go and have a coffee and a cigarette for breakfast together on the deck, the fresh air making your eyes water.

After a brief day in Holland, you take a coach that leaves at seven in the morning from Amsterdam. Everyone is speaking your language and you feel excited. You want to hug everyone just for speaking your language. You listen to their mundane chatter, and you are even more happy to hear ordinary conversations in your language. The travelling hours pass between a heavy, dreamless sleep in which your head droops and your neck becomes sore, and waking up to eat, drink, smoke or pee and discuss the progress of the journey. Many people board the bus in Germany, some refugees returning home, others just visiting. There is no more luggage space for their belongings, packed in large nylon bags, so they have to bring them into the coach and sit cramped in their seats. Most of them are old people, happy to be going home, even though many of them don't have homes to go to. You ask them what they are planning to do, and they talk of families and United Nations programmes and plans to rebuild their houses. You hear that they are mostly building churches and mosques, but houses are not such a priority. Those who are going back for a visit barter with the border guards not to stamp their passports, so that they don't have to explain their apparently illegitimate journeys to the German authorities later. They say something about welfare support. The border guards don't stamp the passports.

Food is shared, stories are told, jokes are laughed at and when you say you live in Britain, they purse their lips and say: 'Oooh, I've heard they have a tough immigration system there.' You laugh at this and don't want to talk about it. You don't want to think about your refugee self at all, you want to enjoy being amongst your people and hearing them talk. You want to forget everything you are leaving behind and sink into your Bosnian-ness.

All border crossings take place in the middle of the night. You stand outside the bus, the bus is in a queue with other buses, and everyone is hopping to keep warm, smoking, and saying: 'Fucking Austrians, they always do this' or 'Fucking Slovenes, they always do this, they just want to get into the EU and pretend they never knew us.' The border guards wear uniforms and serious faces and you remember the Yugoslav authorities who never smiled and always tried to look as fierce as possible. The British police are not as frightening. They don't carry guns, you remember.

You enter Croatia at around 4 a.m. and it feels like the most beautiful moment in your life. The air is a deep bruise-blue, a round moon hangs in the sky and the sea reflects its white light in small ripples. That part of the coast is your favourite, where small barren islands look like mercury dropped in water. The coach pulls into Split station at 10 a.m. and, as the door opens, smells of the sea, fish, coffee and traffic mingle and travel inside. You are taking everything in slowly, separating each scent strand in your nostrils, savouring all of them, even those that would usually make you feel sick. You take your hefty bag and pull its bulk on the ground to the nearest table and order an espresso. The air is warm, the sun is shining and the sky is an endless spread of blue, blending with the sea. You sip your coffee, and then another and another. You are starting to feel giddy with caffeine and the numb exhaustion of the journey falls away into the background. You wash your face in the sink of the cramped white tiled bathroom that smells of urine. You leave your bag in a plastic white kiosk where an elderly lady looks after it for a bit of money, and you secretly hope someone will steal it, but you know no one would

Bluebird

steal such a heavy, cheap-looking backpack. You walk down the buzzing street, among the jewellery and souvenir stands, down into the post office where you buy a telephone card.

'Hello mama!' you say into the small holes of the plastic receiver.

'Darling! You are here! How are you? How was your journey?' Your mother is ecstatic and you are happy to hear that she is so happy.

You dial another number. It's one of your best friends, who doesn't know you're coming. You walk back to the station to board your bus for home, full of memories triggered by almost everything around you, impatience boiling in your chest to get home. The voices of your mother and your friend are still climbing up and down the walls of your brain and you go over the conversations, wondering how you sounded, trying to imagine your own voice in their ears, and wondering if they were thinking about you for as long as you were thinking about them.

People have told you that the city is unrecognizable: 100 per cent damage, which apparently means that every building in the city was damaged. The old bridge is gone, houses are gone, streets are rubble. But you don't want to think about that, not yet. As the bus struggles down the winding road to the valley in which your home town sits, everything looks the same. You also heard that from people. 'When you're approaching, it looks just the same.

Coming home

You can't see any damage.' Two old women are asking you how long it's been since you've been home. You tell them four years and they nod their heads with sympathy. 'It was hard here my dear, you did well not to be around,' one of them says. You agree. The bus stops at the second stop in the city, your stop, and you see your mother waiting for you, craning her neck to see where you are. You get out, take your bag and throw yourself in her arms. You hug each other as if your life depends on it, trying to squeeze as much comfort as you can out of each other, trying to blend into each other. You walk down the street towards your home, and you are struck by something unexpected – everything looks smaller. The streets look narrower, the houses Lilliputian, and you realize you have grown. It is difficult to get a grip on the time that has passed. Everything has been frozen in your memory since you left and now everything is different.

You enter your building and all the graffiti are still there, your name scribbled a thousand times in a child's hand, your neighbour's too. 'Vesna loves Srdjan' or 'Metallica', from the period when your neighbour was into heavy metal. Your heart is beating inside your chest like the heart of a small bird someone once caught and let you hold. You were frightened by its fear and let it escape and everyone got angry with you. The building is spattered with shrapnel holes, like freckles. Outside, the plum tree with the branch where you and the kids from the neighbourhood first discovered the world of adult genitalia is still there. You used to wait in the tree like owls, five or six of you, chatting in whispers and then falling silent, eyes agape, as you spied on one of the neighbours having a shower every evening around eight or nine, visible through the blurry steamed bathroom window. But one night he caught you and screamed: 'Bring me your mothers, if they have nothing to do, I will fuck them!' You all dropped out of the tree, one by one, chicks out of the nest, over-ripe plums smashing on the brown earth, chuckling because he said the word 'fuck', but unhappy – you remember the unease you felt as you belted down the yard with a tight throat – because he used the words 'your mothers' in such close proximity with the rudeness. The idea of his naked body you had watched so many nights in the darkness, the idea of his masculinity, was suddenly a threat and no longer a discovery. Who knows what happened to him, you think.

And then your flat and the doorbell your father installed that chirps like a bird, all the things inside, the view from the balcony, the carpet, the pictures, the absence of your father, the absence of the smell of alcohol evaporating through his pores. There is a shrapnel hole in one of the bedroom walls and your mother says: 'If anyone had been here it would have killed them.' Your neighbour comes knocking on the door and you kiss and hug and hug and hug. He has known you since you were zero, he was born two months before you, he was the first boy you saw having a pee standing up and you wanted to try it too and peed all over your legs. He was the best friend you had growing up, throwing figs at people passing by under your balconies, who then came upstairs to give you hell but retreated once your father answered the door and put his extra-strict face on and then winked at you mischievously. He has known you the longest – only your mother and sister have known you longer – and you think how good it feels that there is someone who has known you for all those years, who remembers you when your milk teeth fell out and you looked like Vlad Dracul, how in England, the place you don't want to remember, in England no one has known you for longer than a few years, no one has known you as just you but as you from Bosnia, you the refugee, you the poor foreign girl: 'Is your family all right?' No one, apart from a few people who are your friends, you realize.

Later on, you go for a walk around the city, and as you step among the ruins you can't believe that this is the same place that you grew up in. The street which was the front line is a ghost now, houses like rotten teeth, dark and hollow. The billion bullet and shrapnel holes make a gloomy relief on the walls. You see small bullet shells on the ground but are too afraid to touch them.

You had dreamed of coming home so often. You had dreamed, usually just as you were waking up in the morning, that you were waking up in your own bed, that when you opened your eyes there would be the old brown wobbly wardrobe packed with clothes, bits of coat sleeves peeking from the cracks between the doors, that you would hear children screaming outside, playing, that your mother would be cooking something in the pressure cooker hissing on the stove, spreading the aroma of beans around the house and that you would get up and the sun would blind your sleepy eyes. And you tried hard to maintain the memories, the smells, the light in your mind, but soon enough the silence and odourlessness of your room would drown everything out and you would get up and try to forget it all again. But now you are here, afraid to open your eyes because it may be a dream again, until you hear your mother talking on the phone in the next room, and smell the coffee and cigarette smoke. You open your eyes and know you're home and the room is real. You feel for your old slippers, and as you try to put them on you see your heels won't fit and that they're now three sizes too small.

Epilogue:
How they met Bill Clinton

The bus to Sarajevo is an old dusty can and on the back seat is a gypsy woman, tattooed from head to toe, offering to read everyone's palm. Next to her is her son who has only one tattoo on his knuckles that reads: S M R T – death. The old gypsy woman looks scary, like someone who might see some bad news on my palm. I don't want any bad news, I've had enough bad news. The bus drags itself up the mountains, crossing from Herzegovina into Bosnia, passing the Neretva river canyon, where the green water is calm, not the rushing jet that it becomes in my home town. The path into Bosnia is uphill a lot of the time and the green forests start to replace the barren Herzegovinian rocks. I see sheep grazing and think of the English animal rights activists and how animals are so free and eat so well here. I say this to my mother who responds: 'Only the people are not so free and don't eat

223

that well.' The whole journey tracks ruins, burnt villages that stand empty, haunted. Folk music plays on the radio and some passengers mouth the words:

> *You have left me, what am I to do?*
> *Why don't you say 'I love you'?*
> *Your eyes haunt me in the night,*
> *I am dying because of your plight!*

Some things never change.

Entering Sarajevo feels unreal. I have seen the city on the BBC, on *Channel 4 News*, but nothing has prepared me for this kind of destruction. The buildings are like broken skeletons, their spines bent towards the rubble heaps beneath. At the station we get a taxi to my aunt's house, my mother doing all the talking. The road is steep up the old cobbled street. As we approach, I see my aunt and uncle standing outside, waving at us. They'd been in Sarajevo all those years, besieged, and their house is hardly standing. The bathroom has no roof, just a plastic sheet with UNPROFOR in sky-blue letters across it. There is no running water, save for an hour or two a day, and that is when they can have a shower or wash the dishes; everything has to be done at an amazing speed if they are to utilize the water fully. Their balcony looks on to a garden with an apple tree and my aunt tells me that she was on the balcony when a shell hit the garden and threw her against the wall and she lost her voice for five days from shock; for five days not a word came out of her mouth, try as she might. She tells me the story and I listen, I picture everything in reels of images: my aunt on the floor, the garden green and burning, she trying to scream for help but silent, no sound emerging from her throat.

One of the worst stories comes from my little cousin who tells it as if it were a joke, laughing all the way through, about how a shell hit the market nearby and a piece of flesh hit him in the ear and he thought it was his eardrum that had fallen out, and all the while a woman who was shell-shocked was walking around in a circle near him, and he was relieved that it was not his eardrum but then realized that it was a piece of this woman's body and that she was bleeding. And he is laughing as he tells this story, for him it seems nothing new, he'd seen hundreds of these things, but I feel like I will never sleep again, afraid of what will come in my dreams.

And every day during my visit in Sarajevo, spending time with my aunt and uncle who love to cook, just before lunch when everyone is having a shot of *rakija* as an aperitif, my aunt tells the same story. She brings out the food, 'Bosnian Pot' – a sort of vegetable stew – places the heavy dish in the middle of the table, and tells us that for so many years they had nothing to eat. They waited for food parcels, she called her sister in Austria, and the sister sent one or two parcels, but nothing much came their way. And she starts to cry, my uncle starts to cry, my mother starts to cry, and I sit silently. Then my uncle tells a funnier (although not funny) story of how they used to sit in the shelter and play dice for hours it seemed, but when they looked at their watches to see how much time had passed, they would find out it was only ten or fifteen minutes since the last time they had checked. And then everyone chuckles a little and I won't touch my Bosnian Pot, my stomach tight from all the stories.

The last day, just as my aunt is about to tell the story again, having brought out the pot with food, my mother says: 'Sister, leave your story for later, my child's going to starve to death, she can never eat after we all cry.' And they all laugh instead and I am a bit embarrassed, but I appreciate the mood change, the clouds lifting from the kitchen table.

So my aunt tells another story, with a big smile on her face. She remembers when Bill Clinton came to Sarajevo and she went to wave the Bosnian and American flags together and take pictures of him. 'How handsome he was,' she says, and my uncle, a professional waiter, boasts about how he served him that time. They bring out the pictures in which my aunt and uncle stand each side of Bill Clinton, two worn-out Bosnians flanking a well-fed American president, all three with enormous hammock smiles suspended between their earlobes.

Acknowledgements

Thanks to Rafael, as always, for everything; to my mother; to Vito for reading when it mattered most. Great big thanks to my agent, Sarah Such, for her help and eternally good advice, and to Sara Holloway for her fantastic editing. Thanks to Bela Cunha, and to everyone at Granta for their work on the book. Thanks to Gabriel, Lilijan, Adele, Almir, Anita, Žana, Čika Mišo, Nicoline, Adam, James, and Paulette for all their support. Finally, everlasting thanks to the Cumbria team who ventured into Croatia in 1992 and to those who offered their homes, help and friendship in my first year in the UK – you know who you are.